Paul Carey Jones was born
Ysgol Gymraeg Melin Gruffydd and Ysgol Gyuun
Gymraeg Glantaf, and read Physics at The Queen's
College, Oxford. He returned as a teacher to Ysgol
Glantaf before embarking on a full-time singing career
in 1998 by studying at the Royal Academy of Music and
the National Opera Studio in London.

He has appeared as a principal guest artist for opera
companies across Europe, and has released three solo
song albums. As a writer he has written articles for the
Wagner Society, the Music Club of London, and the
South Wales Echo among others. His blog *Ranitidine &
Tonic*, much-neglected until a global pandemic wiped
out all his singing work, has at the time of writing just
passed 10,000 readers in 2020. This is his first book.

www.paulcareyjones.net

GIVING IT AWAY

Classical Music in Lockdown
and other fairytales

Paul Carey Jones

To Mam and Dad:
I'll be home soon,
and sorry about the swearing;

and also

to A, E and M:
thank you for having me.

Giving It Away

Acknowledgements

This book is based in large part on my long-running blog, *Ranitidine & Tonic*. I would like to thank all those who have taken the time to read my posts over the years, and especially those who have encouraged me to write more, despite my lack of any natural aptitude for it.

My thanks go to the following people and organisations, in no particular order, who have been of particular help or encouragement, knowingly or otherwise, and my apologies to those who I've forgotten or overlooked: Ashley Kinch, Christian Dowd, Martin Lamb, David Blackburn, Nicholas Chalmers, James Clutton, Wyn Davies, Julius Drake, Polly Fox, Janice Galloway, Anthony Gregory, Alison Guill, David Hicks, Melinda Hughes, Jamie Hutchinson, Kathleen Jones, Mansel Jones, Prof Tegid Jones, Roger Lee, Iwan Lloyd, Stuart MacRae, Stephen McNeff, Oliver Mears, David Moorcroft, Molly Noori, Dr Elizabeth Pounds-Cornish, Gweneth Ann Rand, Malcolm Rivers, Margaret Roche, Kai Rüütel, Brindley Sherratt, Jón Thorsteinsson, Sir John Tomlinson, Mark Valencia, Michael Volpe, Keith Warner, Constance DeWitt, the Arts Council of Wales, and to the Royal Society of Musicians.

Notwithstanding the above, the opinions expressed in this book, and the responsibility for any factual inaccuracies, remain entirely my own.

Diolch o galon a chadwch y ffydd.

Paul Carey Jones
30th October 2020

Contents

Part Three: Orally Fixated

Please note that this book occasionally deals with adult subject matter and, when absolutely necessary, contains language which some may find offensive.

"Estragon: I can't go on like this.
Vladimir: That's what you think."

Preface

I drove to London at the beginning of March 2020, principally for a birthday trip to the theatre with my girlfriend. Over seven months later, I'm still here.

Even at that stage, we were in two minds whether to go out that night, and perhaps if the tickets had been cheaper, and the lure of Tom Stoppard's new play less irresistible, we might have stayed in as a precaution. But with the threat of the pandemic closing in on the UK, we also sensed it would be our last night out for a while. We were right.

Just as I was preparing to head home to Cardiff, the new quarantine guidelines and national lockdown came into force. And so my stay in London was extended.

Ashley is a clinical research nurse, and like most of her colleagues she was immediately switched to working on Covid studies. At the same time, every single one of my singing contracts was cancelled or postponed indefinitely. Staying nearby to help look after Ashley's two children while she focused on helping to find a way out of this mess seemed like the right thing to do. It was *something* to do anyway, at a time when the feeling of helplessness in the face of a global catastrophe was one of the many challenges.

We talked a lot back then about the correct response to these unprecedented times. Ashley suggested we should all be keeping daily journals for the benefit of future generations, like the 17th Century diarists from the time of the Plague. My issue with this idea was that, having kept a diary before, the results were frequently uninteresting and almost always unpublishable, for reasons of both libel and obscenity.

As the days dragged on I started tapping out a couple of blogs, something I'd only ever done sporadically before, which had the virtue of obliging me to keep the content fit for public consumption from the start. For some reason - like its biological vehicle, the mercurial nature of social media virality is shrouded in mystery - the second post, about the lack of sense behind giving away classical music's online content for nothing, caught a fair bit of attention, and the series gained some momentum.

I decided to publish the blogs, along with various other bits of writing, in this format to allow access to those with an aversion to reading on the internet, and to raise some money for a good cause. When I was ill myself in April, the Royal Society of Musicians proved staunch allies, with financial, medical, and moral support, making me feel remembered at a time when so many of us felt forgotten. They neither asked nor expected anything in return, but I hope this can prove something of a thank you at least.

I have, for the most part, left these entries as they were first published on the dates shown, with only minor edits for formatting purposes. You will, I trust, enjoy the moments where hindsight has proved me wrong, and I hope you'll forgive the occasional repetition which results from this approach. But I also trust that the benefits of contemporaneous insights will outweigh any drawbacks, at least in part.

And I also trust that, in publishing these pieces with the other end of this global crisis far from being in sight, I'm not jumping the gun in any way. There is still a long way to go, and many more fairytales to tell.

Lastly, and most importantly, I hope the message my former and future colleagues will take from these stories is one of hope, tempered by realism and caution. To be a professional performing artist for most of my adult life has been a daily dream come true. It will happen again. One day, soon.

Earlsfield, 23rd October 2020

PART ONE

Drilling Holes in the Titanic

Prologue: Waiting for Thanos
17th March 2020

"We're allowed to play but we've got to be careful about the Coronavirus. It started in somewhere called China. A boy ate a bat and got ill. One time at school I vomited in the classroom."

The playground in Tooting Gardens is currently teeming with 5-year-old epidemiologists. It's a sunny mid-March afternoon, I've just had news of another two contract cancellations, and I'm babysitting. I watch M. as she chattily gathers new friends in her habitual carefree manner, at the same time keeping half an eye on my phone as the latest daily updates on the impending COVID-19 catastrophe filter through.

Sitting there, it feels eerily like the dream sequence in *Terminator 2*, where Sarah Connor imagines herself screaming a warning at a similarly frivolous playground, unheeded and too late as a thermonuclear attack arrives and obliterates them all.

On closer examination, that's not quite what this is. A history-changing devastation is about to hit us, seemingly inevitably claiming millions of lives worldwide. Round here they've dubbed it the *Thanos* Virus. And yet, as far as we can see up to now at least, SARS-CoV-2 has a far less egalitarian approach to the souls it chooses to snap away. Whatever the latest measure of the overall mortality rate, it is clearly heavily skewed towards older people, leaving the under-19s almost entirely unscathed. An Angel of Death which passes over the children.

All lives are valuable, of course they are. In the UK the debate rages about the logic of keeping open or closing

3

schools. The received wisdom in other countries seems to be to shut them now, and deal with the consequences as we go along. Every argument in favour of that has validity, as far as I can see.

But this whole thing is a hideous, planetary-wide *Kobayashi Maru* test. There is no right answer, no winning outcome. Merely a card deck of atrocities to be dealt out. A population must consent to be governed, as any teacher who has stood in front of a class of Year 10s knows better than anyone. Telling 7 million teenagers to stay indoors for four months sounds a lovely, straightforward idea in theory. The practice, I suspect, would be rather different.

And really, who could blame them? For years these same kids have been begging those with wealth and power to act on their behalf, to secure their futures and the future of humanity itself, most obviously on climate change, but also on social inequality, job security, house prices, quality of healthcare, and so on – to be told that they don't understand the real world, it's not possible, how could we afford it, calm down and stop being hysterical. Now that their own lives are on the line, those very same adults are making, in an instant and at any cost, many of those previously-impossible changes, and demanding immense sacrifices of every member of society, as usual disproportionately for their own benefit.

Sending a child to their room for a couple of hours is a punishment. At other times, get outdoors we tell them, you need to live a full and healthy childhood. Now they're being asked to put that childhood on hold, for weeks, months, who knows how long. It's not an insignificant sacrifice. Before we feel shocked at any apparent teenage nonchalance about what they've tagged the "Boomer Remover", we might pause to take a broader view while standing in their shoes.

For those of us who are slightly less invincible than the average teenager, an antidote to the incomprehensible stress of all this can be found during an hour or two being lectured by some 5-year-olds.

"Do we need to be scared of the Coronavirus?"

I reply to M. and her new friends that they need to take care and wash their hands properly, but that as children they're very safe and they don't need to worry. Just for once, it's nice to be able to say that without it being a white lie.

17.3.2020

1. Giving It Away
24th April 2020

This thing caught us all unawares. Disney were preparing to launch their new subscription TV channel on March 24th in many European countries, including the UK, just as those countries headed into lockdown. Disney's course of action was clear: they immediately stopped production on their new content, told the content creators they couldn't afford to pay them and laid them off, put all their existing content online for free, and appealed to the public for donations to help them through the current crisis.

Just kidding. Obviously.

What Disney in fact did was to keep producing their new content, increased their marketing, and heavily promoted an attractive offer of around 12% off for early subscribers. Speaking anecdotally, it was more than enough to make me sign up, with the prospect of several weeks stuck in the house and a lot of spare time suddenly looming.

Disney already had a viable business model for home entertainment set up, and so they were well-placed to cash in on a newly captive audience. And it's to mutual advantage: subscribers can stump up £5 a week or so, knowing that their contribution will lead to more of the content that they enjoy. It really doesn't take much – one or two flagship shows in most cases. I'm happy that my contribution to Netflix will help finish *Better Call Saul*, and similarly with NOW TV and *Westworld*.

So where did I get that nonsensical example in paragraph one? Say hello, ladies and gentlemen, to the fairytale world of classical music.

I'm combining separate examples for dramatic effect of course, although there are a few companies who have reacted in pretty much all of these ways. Elements of this response are apparent across the industry – freelance artists have been instantly laid off with minimal or no compensation, the cap has been passed round to the usual long-suffering and endlessly generous supporters, and most bizarrely, vast archives of digital content have been put online for free.

Now, if we are to assume that the current crisis will last a matter of a few weeks, and that we'll all be back to normal by the beginning of the autumn season, this approach might make some sense. But with strong hints over the last few days from the UK and Scottish governments, Angela Merkel, Bill Gates and others, that realistically we need to think in terms of months and years rather than weeks – in other words, well into 2021 if not beyond – the penny should be beginning to drop that the wait to get back to "normal" may be a far longer one. There is even a non-negligible chance that this could be a permanent new "normal".

For companies, a theatrical lockdown which reaches into next year means a long time to go without ticket income, or to rely on audience generosity with nothing to offer in return. For individual artists, it would take most of us beyond the period for which we had confirmed contracts, leaving us without even the support those might have offered, and truly out on a limb.

What then for an industry which has over the last few decades, rightly or wrongly, put all its eggs in the basket of live performance?

This business of releasing digital content free of charge was not without a certain logic, after all. The idea (I infer) was to treat it as a loss leader, to drum up interest (albeit often via a mechanism which was so vague that one suspected it didn't necessarily exist in any genuine detail at all) in buying tickets for live performances – some of which might, with a bit of luck, turn out to be profitable.

But there was always a flaw in the reasoning here. A video recording of a live performance is, in itself, an artistic product, and there was really never any reason why, with some marketing legwork, a viable paying audience couldn't have been built up for it over time. The era when people were used to getting movies and TV shows (as opposed to music – that's a separate set of problems) online for nothing is very much over. If you're not a Disney+ subscriber, and decide you want to watch *Return of the Jedi* on YouTube this evening, it'll set you back £6.99. Would it really take much for classical music audiences to undergo the same paradigm shift?

Almost all of the freelance artists we're watching in those classical broadcasts are currently unemployed and trying to figure out how they're going to survive the next couple of years. Most of them will not be being paid for these broadcasts, and many would have received next to nothing for them in the first place. Would it be too much to ask that we take the opportunity to invite current viewers to contribute to their livelihoods? In fact, had we already done the work to establish the principle of paying for getting classical music on your TV screen, this could have been a genuine boom time for the industry.

Let me give you a concrete example. My YouTube channel contains a song recital playlist, which I made at my own expense a couple of years ago and which, between the various tracks, now has over 10,000 views.

9

While I make no comment on the singer's performance, the quality of audio and video is high, and at, say, 49p a view I could not only make a decent profit, but more to the point have the financial capacity to produce similar content once or twice a year at least – even under the current restrictions on social distancing and so on.

However, the reality is that my huge, and in many cases hugely subsidised, competitors have set the going rate for viewing online classical music content at precisely zero. So I make a loss, and viewers are denied the ongoing production of new high-quality content. It's the artistic equivalent of burning fossil fuel. And as with the boar seller in *Asterix and the Cauldron**, everybody loses.

This moment in history could be an opportunity to think about the most fundamental basis of how our industry works. Without going into the personal details of the Placido Domingo affair and similar recent scandals, a business which sets itself up such that it relies on huge corporate and individual donations, and therefore needs to give them in return, among other things, some special sort of privileged access to "stars" which it is then obliged to create and place in positions of unassailable power, has created an almost-inevitable problem for itself. We lean on subsidies so that a proportion of our tickets can be sold below cost price, allowing the entire industry to adopt a head-in-the-sand attitude to the fact that ours is an expensive product to make. At some point it's surely not a moral outrage to ask those who consume it to pay for it. What might a truly egalitarian opera industry – where audiences are invited to make a grown-up decision to pay for what they're getting – look like?

And let's think again about that expense. Our productions are expensive – but on the scale of television and cinema budgets, not impossibly so, especially if we begin to apply ourselves seriously to the idea of a potential global, at-home paying audience.

When we come to live theatrical performance, there's no getting away from the challenges presented. If we're honest, theatre was already approaching something of a watershed regarding audience expectations of mutually acceptable behaviour and how to share a space in the modern world. Will we need to rethink venues entirely – around a comfort-based individual experience, rather than cramming 'em in? Will theatrical boxes make a serious comeback? Stuart Murphy's latest brainstorm for English National Opera, touting the idea of drive-in opera, raises more questions than it answers. But at least it's a sign that the industry may be willing to go back to first principles, which is surely the least the situation will demand – and this is not to mention how we might configure our singers and orchestra members at a safe distance from each other. Perhaps it'll be like the post-AIDS porn industry, and we'll need medical certificates before we can perform together without protection.

Let's take the worst-case scenario, and say that the idea of staging a show in front of a live audience of thousands is a thing of the past. We'd all take a while to mourn that loss. But as grown-up professional artists, our job is to imagine these scenarios, and prepare to meet these challenges. Opera and classical music on video has almost always been hamstrung by the limitations of pointing cameras at a stage, filming something with the pace and scale of theatre and concert hall rather than cinema or TV. It may be time to revisit seriously what we might be able to achieve by designing pieces from the ground up for screen rather than stage.

Being restricted by the parameters of works designed for theatrical audiences two centuries ago is a choice we make, and other routes are available. If the ideal material to take advantage of a home broadcast format is limited or unavailable, we have a vast number of hugely talented composers, librettists, directors and designers who could produce it afresh. Acting styles might need to adapt, but they always have done in response to the dramatic tastes of the day. In addition, the quality of video and audio equipment people have at home is, in general, unrecognisably superior to what was available when these questions were first being addressed half a century ago. How do we make opera relevant to now? Making it now, for now, is always a good start.

This thing caught us all unawares. We've had a chance to grieve for the art that we've already lost. Take another moment to do so if you need it. But at some point we either choose to give up, or to get our thinking caps on and embrace this grimly terrifying, weird, and yet potentially wonderful new world, and ask whether it holds a place for those who seek to make viable, sustainable, profitable art. Are we up for it?

24.4.2020

*In their quest to repay a debt, Asterix and Obelix capture fourteen boars and take them to market. They pitch up next to an established boar seller, shout him down, and then panic-sell their whole stock for five sestertii, destroying the market value at a stroke. They then realise they have nothing to eat. Their competitor offers to sell them one of his own boars, for five sestertii.***

** It's much more entertaining in the cartoon but I'm no copyright lawyer.*

2. Keeping Going
3rd May 2020

There's a story about the first shadow cabinet meeting after the 1997 UK General Election which has popped into my mind a few times over recent weeks. After eighteen years in office, the Conservatives had just been dealt a thorough drubbing at the hands of the electorate, and met to discuss their strategy options against the newly-formed Labour government. There were a few new faces around the table, brimming with ideas and urgent enthusiasm about how to cut Tony Blair's lot down to size. After a few of them had finished breathlessly brainstorming, Michael Heseltine stretched out his veteran legs under the table, leant back and crooned "Ladies and gentlemen – I suggest we all calm down and pace ourselves. We're going to be here a *long* time." *

Several articles this week have bravely grappled with the concept of socially-distanced theatrical performances, and how they might work. There's particularly good back-of-the-envelope work online from Zach Finkelstein, and others have reached roughly similar conclusions via various configurations. To sum up, you would probably do well to get anywhere near 50% of a regular audience into the usual auditorium space – in reality, something closer to 25% is much more realistic.

That means you'd need to quadruple your ticket prices to hit the same break-even as before – or perhaps you'd only need to double them if you could halve your costs, somehow. If you found yourself in optimistic mood, you might approach the relevant authorities, or a sympathetic sponsor, to subsidise the shortfall.

Even then, for most venues, serious health and safety issues would remain. However successfully we configured the performing and listening space, you'd still need to be able to evacuate people safely in the event of a fire, and show that even without such an emergency, the normal process of getting in and out wouldn't cause any dangerous sub-2m bottlenecks.

The Berlin Philharmonic Orchestra have just bitten the bullet and given their first post-lockdown socially-distanced performance – but note that there was no live audience. One of the things that makes this possible for the BPO is that they have a well-established paid subscription channel, which taps into last week's discussion.

There remains the question of what is a safe distance, and as we learn more about how this virus transmits itself, the news seems to be anything but good, especially for singers and wind players, with revised estimates of safe distancing ranging from 3m to 5m to there being no safe distance at all. The German approach to re-opening churches made particularly sobering reading for my lot, involving an effective ban on singing altogether.

I have no desire to pull the rug from under the huge amount of innovative thinking that's going on – a blank canvas approach to our current challenges can only lead to good things in the long run. But we need to be realistic. As Michael Volpe of Opera Holland Park this week put it with characteristic directness: "Whatever it does, opera (and other art forms) would be best advised not to try to find a way to continue doing the same things in the same way based on half the audience. I guarantee that won't work."

In other words, for all their invention and ingenuity, the various responses to socially-distanced performance are short term solutions at best. Even if they could be made to work financially, under current conditions there would remain a fully justifiable reluctance among many of our audience members to put themselves at risk. What live performance art needs in order to get back to normal lies largely on the medical side of things: better treatments, a reliable system of testing for immunity, and ideally and most importantly, an effective and widely available vaccine.

Now the good news, or grounds for cautious optimism at least. There are signs that even the most sluggish governments are grasping the urgent necessity for widespread testing, and that the technology for reliably doing so is developing quickly. The understanding of effective treatments is deepening all the time. The evidence seems to be moving away from the idea that the virus mutates rapidly, at least to any significant extent (bad news if we were hoping for a miraculously benign mutation, but good news in the hunt for a vaccine), and South Korean researchers seem to have found an explanation for repeated positive tests which doesn't involve the possibility of contracting the illness more than once.

While progress is being made on vaccines at a historically unprecedented rate, we do need a dose of realism about the timescale. Even if an effective vaccine were developed tomorrow, some aspects of the research into potential side effects can't be rushed – for example, there's no way of knowing how it might affect pregnant women in under 9 months – and the process of manufacturing and distributing a vaccine to billions of people in a short space of time has simply never been tried before.**

What the medical scientists have already achieved is staggering, but we need to take on board that they need time, and that is what our lockdowns are for. The sacrifices we as professional performing artists, as with many other walks of life, are being asked to make are huge. On an emotional level we're being denied the activity which keeps many of us sane, and the financial safety net for most of us is minimal, or in many cases non-existent.

But spend ten minutes talking to any healthcare professional working on a Covid ward and you'll know why we're doing it. Every day they watch their patients – not to mention their colleagues – suffer and die, trying desperately to work out why. They come home every night broken. And every morning they put themselves back together and return to the front line.

Every day we can keep going through this buys them the time to save lives. It might well be a while yet. But let's keep going.

3.5.2020

* Admittedly a paraphrase rather than a direct quotation. I'm also deducing it was Heseltine, since the account I read didn't name him – but I distinctly recall him sitting directly facing me in the front row of a Nelson Mass I once sang at the Houses of Parliament, and he adopted that exact pose. He has very long legs.

** Consider also the question of universal uptake of a vaccine. Let's say we establish the infection mortality rate of the virus at around 1% for most groups, as currently seems likely – that's 1% if you catch it. You're then asked to weigh that risk against a yet-to-be-established level of risk of as-yet-unknown side-effects from a rapidly-developed vaccine, for you and your family. It could well be a far from a straightforward decision.

3. Missing You
7th May 2020

You don't get to choose what you're remembered for.

We're sitting and listening to Tim Pigott-Smith at the end of an acting class. He's come in as a last-minute replacement, and has worked through some exercises, leaving the final half hour or so for a relaxed Q&A.

In the nicest possible way he's name-dropping a little, giving examples of memorable performances he's witnessed by great actors. Somehow the topic gets around to acting drunk, and he cites Michael Caine in Educating Rita as the best he's seen. It's Thursday afternoon towards the end of a gruelling week, and despite our enthusiasm, our body language is distinctly low-energy. He mentions that he worked with Caine on one of the worst movies he ever made, set in a World War 2 prison camp. Cogs in the brains of Robert Murray and myself – the two football fans in the class – begin slowly to turn, and then more rapidly to whirr and whizz.

"You're talking about to *Escape To Victory*!"

He was talking about *Escape To Victory*. From that point on the remainder of the session was hijacked, and a first-rate actor with a career spanning decades was obliged to answer questions about Pelé and Ossie Ardiles and John Wark and Sylvester Stallone, to the exclusion of the entirety of his other work.

There's a lesson for young performers I suppose. You should always be careful about signing a contract, since once you've done so and you're out there doing it, people will assume that this is what you do, what you're happy doing, and it may well be what they end up remembering you for, whether you like it or not.

That week of National Opera Studio classes at the National Theatre was unforgettable, and I still lean on many of the lessons learned there today – as well as Pelé's friend, we had sessions with Toby Jones, Erica Whyman, Nigel Planer* and several others. (In one of those situations you'd never foresee before you start out in this odd career, I was called out of Planer's session by a phone call for me at reception, which in fact turned out to be a fake message from the real Harrison Birtwistle who was auditioning upstairs and wanted to hear me. The audition turned out to consist mainly of being photographed beside a table. It's a long story for another time.)

Tim Pigott-Smith, best remembered for his work with Mike Summerbee, was on hand because he was appearing in Eugene O'Neill's three-play cycle *Mourning Becomes Electra* at the NT. I must have been impressed with his session since I went along to see it the following weekend. Tim's character Ezra Mannon died halfway through the second play. Oh, sorry – Spoiler Warning. In opera, he'd have been allowed to take a solo curtain call at the next interval and go home for his tea. The last thing I expected to see was him hanging around for the curtain call several hours later, but sure enough there he was: not even for a solo call, but a regular team-effort company bow. I loved him for it.

Theatre curtain calls always strike me as an affair for grown-ups, although they tie themselves up in as many knots as we in opera do worrying about them. What are they for? Why are they so variable and capricious? Since when and why have audiences started booing the antagonist, and do we ignore it or play up to it or what?

Why can't we all just go home? Do any of these people even remember which character I played?

The most extreme example of the latter question came in Barrie Kosky's production of *The Nose* at Covent Garden in 2016. The entire huge cast, bar the lead, had (almost) identical prosthetic noses fitted, and so we paraded onto the stage at the end in our threes and fours to receive the baffled approval of a squinting public. In fact, after make-up none of us in the cast had much idea who any of the others was either, which was quite a liberating feeling backstage, in the manner of the story about Brian Clough and the Nottingham Forest trainee. **

Singers in the time of Coronavirus seem to have divided into two distinct groups: those who are bombarding their social media friends and followers with daily online performances from their front rooms; and the others who are seemingly struggling to summon the motivation even to maintain their usual practice routine. Extroverts and introverts? There are plenty of performers who fall into both categories, or a combination of each at various times. I wonder how they correlate with those who enjoy curtain calls and those for whom they're an ordeal.

I'm definitely in the latter category. I'm always very clear in my own mind how well or otherwise I've performed, and while I'm glad if I sense an audience has had a good time, it doesn't change how I feel about it. I'd much rather have a one-to-one chat with audience members in the foyer bar afterwards – that's when you get the real feedback. Like any crowd, an audience can't really begin to make sense to you or itself until viewed as a hugely disparate collection of individuals.

But don't go away thinking I don't miss you. Just that it's more about what's happened to us all, the slice of life we've shared together during the performance: it's about the journey rather than the destination. Simon Callow typically puts this far more eloquently than I ever could: "What matters much more is what has passed between us and the audience over the course of the evening. Of course that may involve applause – especially if it's a musical – but even then, it's the minute-by-minute interplay (as often as not silent) that really counts; the sense of communication, the engagement with an audience."

That's exactly what I miss. And, introvert or not, what I'd love to be part of again someday soon.

7.5.2020

* *Nigel Planer's session was the day after Russell Osman's friend Tim's, and upon being told we'd been working with him, Planer described how he'd had to apologise to Pigott-Smith for photo-bombing him at stage door in character as Nicholas Craig. The latter's book 'I, An Actor' is one of the greatest works of theatrical insight ever published, and for one thing coins the term "actoplasm" for the oral emissions of a stage performer – the physical range of which is currently a hot scientific topic.*

** *Clough phoned the training ground and asked to speak to one of the coaches. The teenage trainee who had picked up told him, "You can f*** off." Clough, justifiably incensed, demanded, "Young man, do you know who this is?" The trainee replied, "Yes. Do you know who* **this** *is?" Clough told him he did not. Trainee: "In that case you can definitely f*** off."*

4. Spinning the Wheel
15th May 2020

"Leicester were 5000-1 to win the league but ended up as champions. What are the odds of that happening?"
– Neil Lennon

Les Croupiers Casino, Cardiff, June 1998. For the previous three years I've been working as a schoolteacher, but I'm about to head off to music college, so tonight I'm keeping my cash in my pocket: I'm going to need every penny of it. My colleagues Dave and Iwan, by contrast, are on a roll. Come to think of it I never saw them lose, but I suspect they did so in private; or perhaps my memory has become selective.

Either way, for once they've decided to quit while they're ahead. Having cashed in, Iwan finds a £10 chip in his breast pocket – "for emergencies". Rather than bother the cashier again, he gives it to me and tells me to see what I can do.

I'm a cautious gambler when it comes to my own money, but this is a free hit, so rather than hedge my bets I saunter up to the nearest Roulette wheel and place it boldly on Zero.

Someone else's money, someone else's winnings.* It was worth it for the reaction when I returned only a couple of minutes after setting out, carrying £360 worth of chips. What were the odds of that happening?

Well, that's an easy one: assuming a fair wheel, precisely 36 to 1, or a smidgen over 2.7%.

Watching how people decide to grapple with numbers, and how they apply to our everyday lives, is endlessly fascinating, and the reams of statistics being spewed out during the Coronavirus era so far has provided plenty of opportunity for doing just that. What's the fatality rate of Covid-19, and how might that compare to the chances of dying from other causes, we all want to know? Reading between the lines, I guess we mean, what are my chances of dying from it?

It's really the wrong question. The probability of me dying eventually from some cause or other is 100%. Beyond that, the application of population-wide statistics and probabilities to individual lives is a tenuous affair at best: it's simply not what they're designed for. The half-life of an element can tell you pretty much bang-on what proportion of a large sample of its atoms will have decayed during a certain period. But if you're sat there looking at any particular atom on its own, you're back at the Roulette wheel.

Let's say you're facing a serious medical operation and the surgeon – as they are wont to do these days – informs you that it has a 99% survival rate. That sounds good, you think. 99 out of every 100 patients make it through. But it's hardly any consolation if you're the 1 who doesn't – in fact, it's probably even more annoying knowing how improbable your death was.

A newspaper columnist this week, as part of an argument to send children back to school, quoted 0.03% as the likelihood of dying of Covid-19 for under-18s. Let's for the moment assume that's roughly right. As an individual parent you might think that sounds fine, a chance worth taking. But the only concrete meaning of that number is that, given 10 million or so children of school age nationwide, it translates to the racing certainty of 3,000 deaths (and that's without factoring in the health risk to their teachers). So as a national decision-maker, you might well view that percentage quite differently. Grieving parents would hardly be consoled by the reassurance that their child's death was statistically exceedingly unlikely.

But hang on, I hear you cry – around 15,000 children are killed or injured in road accidents in the UK each year. We don't re-organise our entire lives around that, do we?

Putting aside the question of whether we should look again at the idea that this is a price worth paying for the freedom to drive our own cars, the suggestion that we make no allowance for road safety in our everyday lives is clearly nonsensical. In fact the layouts of our cities are in huge part devoted to allowing for and containing the risk from human-operated vehicles. Imagine for a moment what a town centre without traffic would look like; or perhaps as a more realistic exercise, visualise what a city without human-operated, individually-owned traffic could look like. No need for car parks or parking spaces, far safer junctions and crossings, cleaner air. If we invented the modern automobile today, I suspect no-one would dream of putting one under the fallible, volatile control of anyone who could pass a short test, and allowing them to plough through our midst largely unsupervised.

Be that as it may, it seems we've made about as many concessions to road safety as we're willing to make, and presumably we've decided that 15,000 dead or injured children a year is something we're happy to live with as a result.

Terrorism? The Daily Telegraph recently claimed that "over the last decade, the annual chance of being murdered in a terrorist attack on British soil was about one in 11.4 million per year." I suppose that gives us an average of six deaths a year, and a significant degree of disruption to our way of life.

What about flu, you ask. An average of around 17,000 people in England and Wales have died from influenza in recent years – it's worth noting that this has varied greatly from 2,000 to 28,000 (during the particularly deadly season in 2016). Why are we fretting so much more about the Coronavirus?

In fact, if and (let's all pray) when there's a vaccine for SARS-CoV-2, the precautions against it may well end up looking very similar to our current regime for flu: free vaccines for the most vulnerable, and available to all, and the NHS geared up for a huge increase in hospital admissions in the event of a bad season. Of course, that might change as our medical scientists gather more data and come to a better understanding of how this new virus operates.**

That latter point is crucial, and should underpin every discussion currently taking place on the topic. If you hear anyone speaking with anything resembling absolute certainty regarding any aspect of the current science around Covid-19, please approach with care. The point about all these numbers – overall mortality rates, probability of dying from it, "R0" and so on – is that they require an awful lot of data to establish to any great degree of accuracy, and the gathering of that data in this case is still in its early stages. Plus, they're still strictly speaking only a measure of what's happened in the past, not necessarily an accurate prediction of what may come next.*** Science is the process of establishing and quantifying the degree to which we don't know things. The upshot of that is that there is no such thing as a "scientific fact".

I've left air travel till last. There hasn't been a fatal commercial air accident in the UK since 1989 – so to put it another way, the probability of you dying in a plane crash in this country is currently my lucky Roulette number: zero. The number and complexity of precautions we take when it comes to commercial air travel is immense compared to most other forms of travel.

Grasping the connection between these two statements is the key to understanding the dilemmas surrounding our current crisis.

15.5.2020

* *In fairness to Iwan, he bought us all dinner at Charleston's afterwards. Having been given free rein of the menu, his was the occasion on which I invented the rare fillet steak with onions, mushrooms, peppercorn sauce and a pineapple slice on top. It didn't catch on.*

** *Update October 2020: the Southern Hemisphere has had an unusually quiet flu season - quite plausibly as a result of the same precautions being taken to contain the spread of Coronavirus. The degree to which people will be willing to accept some personal inconveniences to reduce deaths from both flu and Covid-19 once we have a vaccine for the latter will be an interesting discussion.*

*** *I've heard researchers suggest that one of the effects of SARS-CoV-2 might be to turn every carrier into a zombie after 12 months. Presumably it's a reminder that as yet they, and consequently we, have little idea what might be around the corner.*

5. Fine Dining at Fast Food Prices
22nd May 2020

A pair of photos has been doing the rounds this week. One shows the interior of a crowded plane. The other shows a theatre in Germany, with an audience of 200 sitting socially-distanced in a 1000-seat auditorium.

Several singers have shared the diptych, most seemingly under the impression that it provides a watertight case for re-opening theatres immediately.

Meanwhile, the first results of Indigo's *After The Interval* survey of UK audiences were published, and the report makes fascinating reading. In particular, two figures caught my eye. In response to the question "Would any of the following help you to feel safe and comfortable going to an event at a venue again?", the most popular answer was "Limits on the number who can attend" at 76%. Later in the survey, the same audience was asked how, if at all, they'd be willing to contribute financially in order to help companies ensure a successful re-opening after the economic challenges of lockdown. The least popular answer by some distance was "Increasing ticket prices", a mere 18% replying that they'd be up for that.

The two photos were originally posted by my fellow bass-baritone Michael Volle, and the flight seems to have been from Berlin to Wiesbaden (or nearby), where the concert was taking place. It's a short trip, and Germany appears to have its epidemic pretty well under control. Leaving aside the question of why so many people chose to fly a 500km journey (are we really still doing that in 2020?), the implied question of most of the re-posters is: if the plane is safe, how come the theatre isn't?

A more fundamental question might well be: is that plane really safe? Believe me, this is the first time I've ever seen singers point at a photo of a crowded plane cabin and tell us how perfectly healthy it looks. Furthermore, with two-thirds of commercial airlines' fleets reportedly grounded, the idea that it's business as usual for them seems a little tenuous.

(A more pertinent question might be whether bailing out airlines is the best use of public money, when, for example, arts organisations and individual artists could be financially protected for a fraction of the cost.)

As for the sparsely-populated theatre, you'd want to know whether the audience enjoyed it (although since the excellent Mr Volle was singing I'd imagine they very much did), and would they be willing to come back regularly under the same circumstances? Did they maintain social distancing on the way in and out, and would they have been able to do so had there been an emergency evacuation? Does a magic distance of 2 metres really give you indefinite protection from an infected neighbour, even over the course of two or three hours?

And, the bottom line, did they, or would they have been happy to, pay five times the price of a regular ticket in order to be part of an audience one-fifth the size? Everything else aside, you'd assume that at least the airline made a tidy profit on that crowded flight.

The Indigo results suggest that the answer to that last question would be, for most of the UK public at least, an emphatic: No. Even if, courtesy of some Houdini-level contortionism, you could squeeze half the usual audience in and maintain safe distancing, mere double-price tickets wouldn't cut the mustard: for 82% of respondents any increase at all in prices would be unmanageable or unacceptable, despite the fact that almost as great a majority want to see a substantial decrease in audience numbers.

It seems a huge contradiction in terms. Of course I'm being a little unfair – we don't know that exactly the same people answered both questions, and even if they did, were the two factors to be linked more closely in a different survey, the numbers would almost certainly shift closer.

Even so, there's the problem in a nutshell: people want an improved product, but they don't want to pay for it. In the UK it's a particular issue, and not just with the arts. It's at the core of British politicians' problems over the National Health Service, which is free at the point of delivery, funded directly from tax. But for at least a quarter of a century the idea of raising income tax, for example, has been off the table. Even the last Labour leadership, the most left-wing for a generation, was only able to suggest tinkering a little at the upper margins for fear of making themselves electorally untouchable.

As with the British taxpayer, our average British theatre- or concert-goer seems to want a top quality service at bargain basement prices.

How do we in the arts get around this? Within living memory our answer in the UK has almost always been to cut costs, to make the product cheaper and more efficient. But even before this crisis hit, organisations had already cut away most of the flesh, and many had been hacking away at the bare bones for a while too. And the important thing to realise about highly efficient systems is that they are, for the very same reasons, also highly fragile – as the last couple of months have surely proven beyond any doubt.

Perhaps the answer lies elsewhere. In the year I was born, Britain had precisely no Michelin-starred restaurants. Now there are 67 in London alone. Within a generation, a fair number of the British public have been persuaded that an exceptionally good dining experience is worth splashing out on. Not every night or every week perhaps, but once in a while on a special occasion, or to make an occasion special in itself. That's hardly come at the expense of cheaper restaurants or fast food outlets: it's a different product, quite clearly a different concept entirely, and therefore people's expectation of what a reasonable price for it is also instinctively different, without there being a contradiction.

Over the same period, budget airlines have been one of the travel industry's major success stories, and their premium-price competitors have struggled in their wake. Many have taken the classical music approach of attempting to slash their costs, as a result often ending up providing the same sort of experience as their budget competitors, only less well done and still at a higher price. Neither one thing nor the other.

So the rules are different for different products. Consumers view air travel differently from buying food, and buying fast food differently from paying for a fine dining experience. If you saw a fine dining restaurant had cut their costs so drastically that they were charging fast food prices, you might quite justifiably have doubts over the quality of the meal. And whereas you can probably forgive Five Guys for occasionally forgetting the jalapeños, a sub-par fine dining dish misses the point completely.

Let's look again at those two photos. Health risks aside, the plane passengers realised quite some time ago that air travel is not really much fun, and you may as well grit your teeth, get it over with and do it as cheaply as possible. The fun starts when you arrive at your destination.

That's where we come in. In another part of the Indigo survey, respondents were asked how they're currently feeling about the possibility of going to live events again. Only 19% said they'd be comfortable attending as soon as venues are allowed to reopen. It reveals a dangerous gap between our instincts as performers and those of our audiences. I filled in the survey myself – thinking as a potential ticket buyer rather than a professional artist – and was surprised at how cautious most of my answers were. We might do well to bear in mind that a low probability of individual consequences still translates, given a large enough population, to a near-certainty of a number of infections and deaths.

And so we might also do well to take a little time, have a little patience. Our desire as performers to get back on stage, share our art, and make some money is perfectly natural. But we need to make it clear to the public that none of this is worth a moment of risk to their health and lives.

That aside, high art needs to be exceptional, unforgettable, or at least aspire to that. Popular culture aims to entertain you for an evening; we should be aiming to transcend your physical world and change your lives. Fast food versus fine dining. A packed auditorium, under safe conditions so that those present can fully engage in the moment, is no guarantee of that miraculous transformation, but it's surely a key part of a genuine theatrical experience.

So for the time being we need to take every care not to risk infecting our audiences with a deadly disease; and by the same token not to infect the very qualities that make our art worth sharing in the first place.

22.5.2020

6. Living with Covid-19
30th May 2020

Reproduced here is a series of Tweets I sent out on April 19th, soon after recovering from the main symptoms of Covid-19. Day 1 was March 30th – I'm now exactly two months in, and the symptoms have all cleared except for the shortness of breath, which reappeared a couple of weeks ago. Doctors seem to think that should improve slowly, although as they point out there's no way of knowing for certain, since at this stage no-one in the world has had this disease for more than six months.

Since many of you have been asking – here's a brief rundown of my experience of life with "mild" Covid-19. Firstly – I'm alive and feeling almost like myself for the first time in over 2 weeks. I just had a cup of coffee and it was great.

Because I avoided hospital and pneumonia, technically my case was mild. In reality, it was anything but. I've had shellfish poisoning a couple of times, and the closest analogy is that it was as bad as that, but in slow motion over a couple of weeks rather than a couple of days.

Days 1-3 were a mild cough. Day 4 I made chicken soup at lunchtime and then collapsed into bed just feeling hot and exhausted. Day 5 I perked up again.

Day 6 was when it really hit – a proper fever (38-39 degrees), extreme fatigue, cough deepening causing an inability to breathe properly.

Day 7 those symptoms worsened, and on Day 8 I was in trouble – my breathing had quickened and shallowed, the fever wouldn't shift and I was alternating between shivering and sweating uncontrollably. Extreme fatigue and drowsiness, and almost complete loss of appetite.

My heartbeat was rapid and erratic, and blood oxygen levels getting towards dangerously low levels. I had a bag packed for hospital at this point.

I got some antibiotics for the cough – to cover any possible bacterial infection – via NHS-111. Hard to know whether they helped – I did seem to produce a bit of gunk once they kicked in, but the fever remained persistent.

Day 9 was a bit better and just enough to keep me out of hospital. I was still struggling with fever, extreme fatigue and drowsiness – sleeping 18-20 hours a day – diarrhoea, nausea, tingly skin, and more than anything with breathing – it felt impossible to get enough oxygen.

Day 10 – 14 were very similar, with the symptoms seeming to take it in turns to give me a proper going-over. As soon as one aspect improved, another would kick in. The impossibility of getting into a rhythm of being ill was one of the things which made it so exhausting.

At this point my partner was also down with Covid, and with two kids at her home we were grateful for the stockpiling – and the emergency supply package from the amazing Melinda Hughes.

Day 12 (Good Friday) I got seen by a GP at a special Covid hub centre – the effort of getting dressed and driving over there made me feel like I was going to collapse. But my oxygen levels seemed good – and improved with mild activity – and my chest sounded ok. Reassuring.

I'd had a constant fever for over a week by now, and I was beginning to have trouble working out what was going on. I've been watching Breaking Bad, and kept waking up thinking the house was surrounded by police and worrying about where all my illicit dollars were stashed etc.

From around Day 16 onwards things began slowly to pick up. The diarrhoea had eased, although my appetite was still non-existent, & there were periods where my temperature dropped to near-normal. I began to go for short walks around the block after dark, which felt like marathons.

That gradual improvement continued. This is now Day 21, and I've been more or less fever-free without paracetamol for three or four days now. My breathing feels almost normal, the cough is a lot better, and I'm only sleeping for 12 hours a day or so.

So I'm almost feeling myself again. Hope that's useful and answers a lot of your questions.

Bear in mind, all this comes under "mild symptoms". In reality it completely wiped me out for two weeks and more. Worth considering when we're thinking about the practicalities of lifting lockdowns etc.

PS advice re preparing for getting hit: do stockpile! Think about a week or two where you really can't go out, how would you cope? Especially if you've got kids, pets, dependents etc.

You'll need a lot of paracetamol – two weeks' worth is 7 packs of 16. (Bear in mind you can only buy two packs of pain killers at a time.) Think about where you're going to ride this out. You'll need a lot of comfortable, loose clothing – because of fever sweats I was having to change clothes 2 or 3 times a day at some points. Get a desk fan.

You'll also need lots of fluids – 2-3 litres a day, and you probably won't feel like eating or drinking anything. Keep track of how much you're drinking. Get a reliable thermometer and a blood oxygen monitor if you can.

Most importantly, do NOT get sucked into the nonsense of "battling" the illness, carrying on as normal, stiff upper lip and plough through it etc. This isn't a war. Get yourself organised, cancel everything and go to bed. You fight a virus lying down.

For some context – because I avoided hospital I haven't been tested, but my partner tested positive on Day 4 of my symptoms, so in my case we're 99% certain.*

I'm mid-40s and otherwise fit and healthy, and I do breath control for a living. Those breathing exercises really do help and I can't see any harm in starting now if you can stand it.

I hope that proves useful to someone. If anyone has any further questions please don't hesitate to drop me a line. Singers in particular may find an excellent online article by Molly Noori, titled "Can I Sing Yet?", of interest for further reading – the pattern of her symptoms is remarkably similar to mine.

* Update: in late August I tested positive for antibodies, confirming that this was indeed Covid-19. By the time of writing the symptoms and after effects have all cleared, and I feel back to normal - whatever that might be.

7. Freelancers and Impotence
4th June 2020

Sir Arnold: Power goes with permanence.
Sir Humphrey: Impermanence is impotence.
Sir Arnold: And rotation is castration.
– Yes Minister, Jonathan Lynn and Anthony Jay

"If you saw it, then why didn't you report it?"

It's a good question. A friend has recently moved to a new job in the classical music world, and has just had her eyes opened to the industry's not-so-proud tradition of sexual harassment for the first time. It's not the first thing she asks me. The first thing she asks me is,

"What the fuck is the matter with all these wankers?"

Another good question, to be fair.

As the conversation continues, she asks if I've ever witnessed any such behaviour myself. The honest answer is only once, kind of.

I'm sitting in an armchair in a dressing room at a major opera house. Watching the clock, trying not to watch my colleague changing. She's asked me to be here as some sort of chaperone/bodyguard – there must be a technical term for it, but I skipped most of my music theory exams – since a senior colleague in a position of authority has been doing the rounds of the dressing rooms, conveniently enough always during the point in the female singers' pre-show routine where they're in their underwear. Make-up, wigs and costumes often have to go on in a particular order, so changing the routine isn't an option. Neither is locking the door –

43

they can't be secured from the inside, and anyone backstage seems to be able to get in if they want to. Sure enough, regular as clockwork, here he is, slightly taken aback to find his quarry with company. He takes it in his stride, courteous and charming, although I am not charmed. The rest of the evening passes without incident. I perform the same function twice more, and for the final performance (I've flown home by this point) she arranges for another trustworthy friend to be present. She later relates that the Lothario appears to realise what is going on by now, but again, all passes without further incident and that's that.

That's as close to first hand as I've ever been. I'm lucky: as a heterosexual man, I'm almost never on the receiving end of sexual harassment, and if I have been then I'm almost certainly too stupid to have noticed.

Why didn't I report it? I think about it a lot.

Firstly, I didn't really witness anything untoward – my presence was intended to prevent that, and it worked. So in itself my testimony wouldn't add up to much. Secondly, my colleague didn't want to take the matter any further, and it was her story to tell or not, as she saw fit. Had she decided to pursue it, I hope I'd have been brave enough to back her up.

But the truth is, I'd have to take a very deep breath before reporting any such case. And that's because I'm a freelance artist, and potential victim of harassment or not, I'm dispensable, and therefore vulnerable.

In her scintillating book *Opera, or the Undoing of Women*, Catherine Clément speculates that the reason opera houses so often demand that their prima donnas are foreign is less to do with the lure of the exotic, and more about removing them from their native environment and support network, increasing their vulnerability and ensuring they don't get too powerful. As with most of her more compelling hypotheses, it applies to all singers, not just her fragile divas. Like any singer, I've occasionally been on the end of some pretty rancid behaviour, and when it's happened abroad all I've wanted to do is get home safely in one piece. The idea of pursuing justice and correction is a long way from my mind.

There does appear to be a rule of thumb the world over that a huge number of singers rarely, if ever, appear at their "home" company. It's a global art form, and there's generally a glut of supply, so casting directors have a whole planet of singers to choose from. But you do look at some cast lists, taken over an extended period, and wonder at the absence of local talent. Audiences, meanwhile, often don't seem to realise that singers don't get to choose where we sing – we have to wait to be invited.

My colleague Josef was an exception, having appeared regularly as a freelance guest artist for his home opera company with great success. After many years of dedicated service, he moved to live elsewhere. Before leaving, he took the trouble to tell the company's director (a non-native) that he'd be delighted to come back any time he could be of use to them, since appearing there meant so much to him. He was told that he should be grateful for what he'd been given. He hasn't been invited back since. The colonial masters have spoken.

My point is, a singer who finds herself the target of harassment at work might first turn to her fellow cast members for support, only to find that they are in many ways as vulnerable as she is – freelance visitors, far from home, interchangeable and dispensable, however

45

willing they are to help. Increasingly this may even apply to the chorus, and sometimes even the orchestra too.

This wasn't always the case. The last remnants of it have all but died away in the UK, but a generation or two ago, opera houses had a backbone of permanent company principals: a genuine company of artists. Far easier, with that far greater degree of security, for singers to call out bad behaviour by colleagues, or to support them when they're the victims of it. Not that sexual harassment wasn't prevalent in the old days... but if anything our current situation makes it even harder to deal with.

Might we return to such a system? The answers to our current problems surely lie ahead of us, not behind, and even before this extraordinary crisis, the world had changed. Aside from anything else, permanent singers cost a UK company more than freelancers, with National Insurance, holiday pay, pensions and so on to be thrown into the mix. Our new friend Rishi Sunak has been one of the more impressive members of the government during the current crisis – admittedly that's leaping over a bar which is not so much low as subterranean – but you sense his largesse might not last much longer, and already fresh rumblings about the supposedly privileged status of the Self Employed have been emerging from his direction. Canny employers will be looking closely at the fine detail of the IR35 legislation in preparation for potential battles ahead.

However, we face more urgent problems. The state will, we hope, at some point soon step in to ensure that our most valuable arts organisations and institutions don't go bankrupt and disappear forever. But as freelance musicians, we rely entirely on performance fees as the

46

mechanism for passing on the industry's funds to us. In an era where few if any of us are permanently affiliated to a company, when those companies aren't giving performances, how can the industry accurately target support for us too? Assuming that safeguarding our futures is considered as important as doing the same for buildings and administrative staff, that is.

No one made much fuss while it was happening, but perhaps companies are also beginning to realise what they lost when their permanent principals were quietly allowed to drift away without being replaced. The recent situation at the Royal Opera, where a performance of *Don Carlo* had to be cancelled since there was no cover for the lead soprano, and no time to fly anyone in from elsewhere (international opera's addiction to carbon-intensive solutions to foreseeable problems is a topic for another time), would never have happened in the old days, old lags assure me, when there would have been several Elisabettas in the House at any one time.

Given time, any system will eventually expose its own flaws. It's all very well taking down a figurehead like Placido Domingo, but if you leave intact the system that allowed him that amount of unchecked power, you've achieved nothing. Domingo should know that well enough himself, given how often he's been on stage at the end of *Tosca*; even when Scarpia dies, the soprano still loses.

Power corrupts, and positions of unsupervised power will tend to attract those who are least well-equipped to resist the corruption. It's entirely right that the accusations against him were taken seriously and that he faces the consequences, but once the dust settles it's the system that produced and enabled Domingo which needs closest examination. Any industry which allows

47

as a matter of course, for example, a situation where certain male artists are only allocated male wardrobe and make-up assistants, keeping female employees well away from those dressing rooms for their own protection, has more fundamental problems than the behaviour of one individual, however prominent.

"If you saw it, why didn't you report it?"

Power goes with permanence. This job is, has somehow become, my life. I hate it and I love it and I can't live without it. Every time I stick my head above the parapet, I risk losing that: casting is a subjective process, and choosing one singer over another for a role, whatever the real reasons, cannot be challenged and requires no justification. I'm expendable. I know it. They know it. They know that I know it.

Impermanence is impotence. I'm scared to speak up. I want to work. I want the conductor, director, casting director, designer, critics, sponsors, audience, colleagues, company managers, chorus, wardrobe assistants, the guy who does the stage door night shift and the taxi driver on the way home, to like me. Because I want to be invited back. To be a freelance artist is to live your life like a startled rabbit, constantly checking for potential danger to your career. I want to help, to be an ally. But above everything else, I'm scared, an addict terrified of being denied his drug.

Rotation is castration. What would change that? Is there a way to keep us in one place for longer? To feel we belong, so that we can set the standards, draw the lines? To allow some of us to put down a few roots for once? Give us permanence, and with it will come the power to speak out. Then, perhaps, some of us might be able to help. If we're brave enough.

4.6.2020

8. Opening Up
15th June 2020

Strong reactions emerged over the weekend to leaked reports that the UK is about to allow orchestras and choirs to return to work, with severe conditions of 3-metre distancing and limits on numbers in the same room (eight instrumentalists, or six singers). It's struck a nerve coming at the same time as flights are resuming and shops are re-opening. If it's safe to go to Primark, why can't we be allowed to make music properly?

I fully understand – and share – musicians' frustrations, especially when so many of us have been left in the financial lurch by the eccentric gaps in the UK government's support schemes. We need to get back to work. But we also need to take care. For one thing, sitting in the same room with colleagues for several hours at a time is clearly not an equivalent situation to spending twenty minutes whizzing around a large shop. (Although spare a thought for the shop workers on their long shifts.) The time element of viral load continues to be overlooked in favour of distance, but it's at least as vital.

Evidence continues to emerge that asymptomatic carriers are major spreaders of the virus, and so relying on self-reporting or temperature checks isn't enough to ensure safety. This isn't just a case of trusting your colleagues not to turn up and cough all over you.

Furthermore, as the increasing advice to wear masks should tell us, the sense that the spread of the virus takes place in the air at least as much as it does via surfaces is strengthening almost daily – although this might be much clearer if our politicians allowed themselves to admit the possibility that they got it wrong at the start. And other signs show us that this may be, above all, an indoor virus.

Perhaps, despite all that, we're willing to take the risk. That may well be our impulse now, but professional orchestras do tend to be acutely aware of even relatively minor health and safety risks to their members – and quite rightly so. Would hacking away at the safest scientific advice in the interests of an early return to work really stand up to that level of scrutiny?

As I've discussed before, a health risk of, say, 1% might seem negligible to us as individuals. But put 1000 people in an auditorium, and that translates to the near-certainty of an event – not necessarily exactly 10 people each time, but even if we're lucky and it's only one, try picking out the unfortunate individual whose health or even life you think is worth sacrificing. The Indigo audience survey showed clearly that our supporters have misgivings about the safety of returning to venues too soon. We need to earn their trust, and sending out the message that our livelihoods take priority over their health is not the way to do that.

It will continue to be increasingly frustrating for us to watch colleagues in other countries return to work earlier than us, reaping the rewards of more competent governments, many of which have also been far swifter and more generous in their financial support of the arts.

But we can't fight facts, and the worst approach to opening back up would be to lurch through a tentative first step and then swiftly have to take two backwards. To get through this, we need to get the virus under control nationally. We need an effective system of rapid testing, so performers and audiences can sit together knowing that they aren't infecting each other. And in

50

the meantime we need financial support to ensure we're all still here ready to go when it's safe to do so.

The remedies are clear, but they're not easy nor painless to apply. Frantically searching for less gruelling alternative treatments is, I respectfully suggest, a waste of time and energy. Let's buckle up and take the medicine.

15.6.2020

9. Fiddling While Rome Burns
24th June 2020

The crisis in the UK theatre industry really began to bite this week, with the continuing lack of clarity from the government having an increasingly tangible impact. In one of the biggest shocks so far, the Theatre Royal Plymouth announced that they were making their entire artistic team redundant with almost immediate effect.

One of that team was Production Assistant Lauren Walsh, who posted a must-read thread on her Twitter account. The whole thread is available online – please do take the time to read through it. I've reproduced the first part of Lauren's thoughts below.

"I'm one of the artistic team. This week I was told I'll likely be made redundant. I asked what the prospects were for me being rehired in any capacity further down the line. The response was that any new hires would be unlikely, possibly for up to two years. I'm from a working class background. It took me a really, really long time to get my foot in the door of the theatre industry. I worked so hard, and even then it only came together thanks to a bursary placement from Jerwood Arts. I feel bereft. There's no funding available, so making my own work is nigh on impossible for a while. Most other theatre organisations are in a similar position in terms of redundancies and won't be hiring either. I have no idea where to go. I can't see any way of remaining in the industry. I don't have savings. I don't have a safety net or a family home I can go back to. And now, thanks to my landlord responding to my message about redundancy by telling me she was increasing my rent, I don't have a home. I'm not posting for pity.

I'm trying to highlight what people mean when they talk about the impact C-19 will have on diversity in theatre. It's working class people who will have to move on. It's black people. It's Asian people. It's disabled people. It's LGBTQ+ people. The upper/ middle classes who've held the positions of power in theatre for so long will continue to do so. And we'll have to fight our way back in all over again."

There's a lot of talk about diversity in the arts. A major part of any meaningful campaign to increase diversity has to involve doing the hard, long-term work of increasing access to arts training in state schools. Talk is cheap, and too often politicians and industry leaders pay lip service to an inclusive approach, and yet fail to go beyond a bit of window dressing, neglecting the investment at grass roots level without which the path to a career in the arts will continue to get steeper for those from less privileged backgrounds.

The present danger is that in our eagerness to save theatres and orchestras, buildings and institutions, we lose sight of the individual artists required to make those places mean anything. The charge levelled against funding for the arts – that it's taxpayers' money paying for rich people's pastimes – could be countered in no better way than channeling some of those funds to make sure that working class artists like Lauren aren't lost to the profession forever. Let's bear that in mind as we lobby our politicians and public.

In the long term, the low pay and precarious instability of most artistic careers are barriers to inclusivity. There are dangerous rumblings that artists' fees will have to be cut in order to help theatres stabilise themselves financially. Every time that path is taken – and it's an easy one since there's almost always more artists than work – artists are effectively being asked to subsidise their own industry. That's an option only available to those from wealthy backgrounds, or with other sources of finance. Employers should be in no doubt that every time they take that soft option, they are decreasing diversity, as well as gnawing at the vital organs of their host animal. We're at a crunch point in the UK where we need to decide whether we're serious about some of these art forms as professional ventures – or are we really happy to revert to what are essentially am-dram models?

There's a deep and urgent need for more long-term stability for artists in my own branch of the business, and there's no doubt that the lack of paths to a reliable income is another barrier in the way of any artist from a low-income background seeking a career. We need to find ways of moving away from the ultra-Darwinism of an exclusively freelance model, because it leads to survival of the least vulnerable rather than the fittest.

None of this is to undervalue the contribution artists from more privileged backgrounds make to their various crafts. But we would unarguably be far poorer for a lack of working class talent streams. Acting needs its Ray Winstones and Idris Elbas. Opera needs its Tomlinsons and Terfels. Their potential successors are in an incredibly vulnerable position. They need help, and quickly.

24.6.2020

You can follow Lauren's Twitter feed at @lozzF_W

10. Opera's *Kobayashi Maru* Test
29th June 2020

"Your scientists were so preoccupied with whether or not they could, they didn't stop to think if they should."
– Dr Ian Malcolm, *Jurassic Park*

The Guardian ran an article last week from Alex Rushmer, the owner of *Vanderlyle*, a restaurant in Cambridge, explaining why, despite the UK government's decree that businesses such as his can reopen from July 4th, he'll be staying shut. (23rd June edition - "Here's why we won't be opening on 4 July".)

He cites three issues: the unpredictability of potential quarantine closures should a staff member or customer test positive; the financial viability of operating with 30-50% capacity because of social distancing; and the essential quality of the whole experience under current conditions.

Back in the opera world, the government's advice for performing venues is even more vague and perplexing than that for restaurants. Theatres and concert halls can reopen, but not put on live performances. Eh?

Nevertheless, glimmers of bright ideas continue to emerge. English National Opera are at the forefront of the opening-up debate, outlining plans for a socially-distanced opera season in the autumn, with the reduction of the recommended safe separation to 1 metre allowing them to operate at 48% audience capacity, or so they say. This would replace their much-postponed production of *Hairspray*, and the fact that they seem to have realised, whether by accident or design, the inherent contradiction in an opera company asking for taxpayers' money in order to stage a commercial musical is to be welcomed. No government, and this one least of all, would require much of a second invitation to pursue that train of thought to its logical conclusion. With any luck, ENO will be employing opera singers later this year, and that has to be a good thing.

If any company is well-placed to strike out into the "New Normal", it may indeed be ENO. The cavernous Coliseum has always been something of a mixed blessing for the company, but all that space should be a clear advantage when it comes to socially distancing an audience, and 48% capacity is still well over a thousand seats there. A glance at their accounts for recent seasons suggests that the box office has accounted for around 20% of their overall income, so a reduction in ticket sales should prove less of a problem for their business model than for some other companies.

That seems to bode well for addressing two of Alex Rushmer's restaurant issues at least. If the government and/or sponsors can somehow be persuaded to make up the ticketing shortfall, perhaps there is a non-ruinous or even near-viable financial model here, in the short term at least.

How about the quality of the experience? ENO have mooted chamber-style performances, with limited numbers of performers on stage and in the pit, and a thrifty approach to production costs. This is where the Coliseum's size may be less of an advantage, but will at least be interesting to watch, especially for those of us who occasionally query the sanity of an industry where often more is spent on the costumes than on the performers wearing them. Is all that really necessary? I guess we're about to find out.

Furthermore, with British singers sitting at home enviously twiddling our thumbs as we watch our colleagues in other parts of Europe get back to work, they'll be spoilt for choice as never before when it comes to casting. So there's every reason to suppose that the quality of the singing will more than make up for any austerity on the visual side of things.

"Logic? My God, the man's talking about logic; we're talking about universal armageddon." – Dr Leonard McCoy, *Star Trek II: The Wrath of Khan*

On the general subject of getting show business back on the road, what hasn't been discussed anywhere near as much as these other two aspects is the third issue in the Guardian piece, which is the potential for disruption from the virus itself. According to the NHS' Test and Trace guidelines, the approach seems to be that if anyone comes into contact with an infected individual, they are required to quarantine for 14 days. It's not clear what constitutes "contact" in this context, but one positive case would presumably lay waste to any carefully planned rehearsal schedule. And then throw 1000 members of the public into the mix at a performance... The potential for chaos is immense, and it's already causing problems in other countries.

One suggestion of a relatively low-cost way in which the government could help get us back on stage is for them to provide regular testing for cast and crew members, as has been happening (presumably at their own expense) with professional football teams. It seems like an alluring solution, but the devil is in the detail: even given high priority, we could expect a 24 hour wait for results. So, for example, we might test everyone on Sunday morning ready to start rehearsals the next day – and then repeat every couple of days, with a day off each time to wait for results. Or perhaps given an even bigger budget, we could have a rolling system of tests every day, although professional singers might soon tire of an invasive naso-pharyngeal swab at the start or finish of every rehearsal.

Bear in mind that the data on the reliability of tests when applied to non-symptomatic patients is still limited – understandably, the focus for most countries has been on testing those with symptoms, and the most severe ones at that. So it's not at all clear how accurate pre-emptive tests are for those without symptoms are at the moment. It would only take one false negative to really put the cat among the pigeons.

On top of that, the "bubble" demands being made on footballers are strict, essentially taking over every aspect of their lives – would singers be willing or able to put up with that? And if not, or they got it slightly wrong, would a company then risk having to suspend them, as Watford did with three of their players at the weekend? (Worth noting perhaps that, even though footballers are more readily replaceable than singers, Watford still lost their match.)

And then, what happens to a singer in the case of a positive test? If they have to quarantine for two weeks, and miss a string of performances, under our current system of remuneration, they don't get paid, at all. To make such a system work in the UK you'd need to rethink the whole freelance model – which isn't a bad idea for many reasons, but you'll forgive me if I don't hold my breath.

The closer you look, the deadlier you realise the minefield of even the known-unknowns is. On balance I'm heartily glad that I'm only watching from behind the barbed wire, rather than trying to plot a course through it as our industry leaders are obliged to, even though it means I'm stony broke as a result. It must be tempting, even perhaps the only vaguely sane financial option, to consider the Southbank Centre's suggestion of battening down the hatches in the hope of riding out the storm until a full reopening is possible. Could they reopen in a more limited way in the meantime? Maybe. Should they? Probably not.

But it's a *Kobayashi Maru* test, and the fact is that we need the more intrepid space cadets to succeed. The current crisis has exposed in most brutal fashion the systemic flaw where classical music relies entirely on live performances to distribute funds to a huge proportion of its most valuable artists. *Vanderlyle* has a fallback option of operating as a takeaway-only restaurant for the time being. Freelance musicians have no such Plan B. So even those of us who are very rarely on the radar of ENO's casting department need its approach, and others like it, to pay off.

And I suspect that it has more chance of shaking the government into some sort of action – a concrete proposition would at least force them into a Yes or No answer. It surely beats sitting around waiting for them to reveal their masterfully elaborate rescue plan: as with almost every other aspect of this crisis, it must be pretty clear by now that there isn't one.

Too little, too late? It would be better than nothing at all.

29.6.2020

11. Drilling Holes in the Titanic
3rd July 2020

It's surprising what you don't miss. I was last in a pub on my birthday, and if you'd told me back then that almost four full months later I wouldn't have been in one since, I'd probably have been quite glum. As it is, I can't honestly say I'm pining for a pub crawl, although I certainly would like to spend a few hours with many of the people with whom I used to go for a pint. And come to think of it, I suppose I miss having enough money to go to the pub. But the sight of sweaty crowds on the streets of London, paying £6 a pop to drink beer out of milk cartons and plastic bottles, and then using alleyways as urinals, has brought the point home: was it ever that much fun anyway?

It's Friday 3rd July and in England, the pubs are reopening tomorrow, while theatres and concert halls are remaining resolutely shut. As with aeroplanes a few weeks ago, many of my exasperated colleagues are asking: if pubs are deemed safe, how can a theatre not be?

My dear friend Brindley Sherratt has pithily suggested that we hire a 747 and perform an opera in the fuselage, highlighting the absurdity of the current situation. Our frustration is understandable, as we read daily reports of theatres closing or laying off staff, and we watch our own resources of finance and enthusiasm dwindle. As individuals and an industry, we can't take much more of this.

But debating the relative safety of flights, pubs, theatres and various other set-ups is missing the point, and by arguing on that basis we risk spiking our own guns. Back in March, Tomas Pueyo described the strategy for tackling this pandemic as having two stages: the Hammer – where we go into a strict lockdown to bring the infection down to a manageable rate; and the Dance – where we loosen up in various stages in order to keep the much-discussed basic reproduction number, R0, below 1.

He uses the metaphor of a dance, because there is inevitably a degree of slow-slow-quick-quick-slow in all of this. As society opens up, the chaotic nature of how a virus spreads will inevitably lead to further outbreaks which are localised and unpredictable. The measures to counteract that have to be agile. So the bottom line is not whether, for example, pubs or shops or cinemas or theatres are safe. None of them are entirely risk-free under the current circumstances. But how quickly can they be shut back down if necessary with minimal notice?

To some extent it's also a question of priorities, and there can be no denying that theatre and live music are clearly further down the government's pecking order than beer and football and Primark. But it's equally clear that it's harder when it comes to performing arts venues. We need time to plan, prepare, rehearse and launch – months rather than days or weeks. Smaller-scale operations might be a bit more agile, and generously subsidised ones may have more options on the table. But ultimately they all need time and stability, to a far greater extent than a pub or a cinema.

It's tempting for us as individual performers to clutch at straws and demand immediate employment at whatever cost. But what the industry needs is long term clarity. A rush to open up, even if theatres could reopen now with a limited number of seats, would in most cases deepen their financial problems rather than solve them. It costs just about as much to put on a show for a

30% capacity crowd as it does for a full house, so in reality we'd merely be drilling a few more holes in the hull of the *Titanic*. Online performances and recitals to empty halls are far from unhelpful, but they don't solve the immediate problem that the industry's ecosystem depends on a full range of viable live performances.

So in fairness to the UK government, their approach to emerging from lockdown isn't as slap-dashedly inconsistent as it may seem, although they are spectacularly bad at explaining it – their shifty reticence with the data, and the sidelining of their scientific experts, hasn't helped them at all in that. To judge from the reactive nature of their approach to the entire crisis, perhaps a few nudges in the right direction might help them nail their colours to the mast, as discussed earlier this week. But that also begs the question of the risks involved: lurching backwards to another round of shutdown cancellations would be disastrous. A Treasury-backed insurance scheme would be one reasonable way the government could help. At the very least, their "roadmap" needs some dates and numbers on it.

For better or worse, as a society-wide project, post-lockdown opening up has to be government-led, and we're stuck with this lot, their priorities and their decisions. Politicians in a modern democracy are inevitably obliged to think in simple terms, and so questions need to be put to them in a simple way. Complaining about airlines and pubs and football gets us nowhere.

What we need to know right now is: when can we get back to work? What will the exact restrictions on audience capacity be? What happens if we have to shut back down? And how are we going to survive till then?

3.7.2020

Update July 2020: the government has helpfully provided a case study in its latest U-turn, tonight deciding that village cricket can after all go ahead from next week, having stated it was unsafe earlier today. Has the science changed in the last few hours? It seems unlikely. Rather, in the face of public pressure, they've decided that the change of heart is worth the cost of adding another smidgen onto Ro (and also knowing that it won't be particularly problematic to reverse that decision if necessary later).

12. The Death of British Opera
6th July 2020

Three cheers for Oliver Dowden. He pulled through. Or at the very least, he and our new friend Rishi Sunak – still artists' favourite Tory, for whatever that's worth – have mimed signing the cheque that should ensure that there's some sort of UK performing arts industry next year.

Thus a short and rare period of artistic solidarity comes to an end, and rather than unanimously attacking the government for its ineptitude and inaction, we can safely return to the comfortable familiarity of attacking each other, as the winners and losers of the self-styled New Deal emerge.

As the dust begins to settle and the smoke of the valedictory fireworks clears, there already seems to be a little less to celebrate for the artists themselves. When it comes to supplying funds to the army of freelancers who are at the core of how the UK arts actually function, the secondary rumblings from the government are less promising.

In truth, who can blame them? They've fulfilled their side of the bargain: a huge cash injection into the top of the machine. If they don't feel it's their job to fix the mechanism via which the industry chooses to distribute those funds to the people who actually produce the material which is the entire purpose of the whole endeavour, they may well have a point.

I'll take opera singers as a case study, since that's where my own experience lies, but the same arguments apply to many other branches of the UK arts where the artists themselves are almost all employed on a freelance basis.

The hard fact is that not only are we artists not getting any of that funding right now, but most of that money is going to be given to people whose job it is to prevent as much of it getting to us as possible. Because in the modern UK arts industry, artists are not employees: we are the raw material. And part of the job of those selling the product is to keep the cost of the raw material to a minimum.

I don't blame any individual in any of those jobs. In their shoes I would be doing exactly the same. It's literally what they're paid to do, and many of them are far more enlightened and benevolent than they have any need to be. This is a criticism of the system, not of the individuals within it. In many cases, we're lucky to have them.

And indeed as individual artists, we ourselves have been complicit in our own predicament. In fairness, when choruses and orchestras have been made redundant or had part-time status imposed upon them, action has often been taken, at least making a point and taking a stand of sorts. But a generation ago, solo singers accepted the gradual disbanding of permanent company principal status with barely a murmur, perhaps eyeing the opportunity to steal a march on our closest rivals and move up a rung or two in the pecking order.

Let's wake up and smell the coffee. The recipients of the government's unexpected largesse – our prospective employers – are no more likely to find a way to distribute some of their pot of gold to us than Tim Martin is going to offer to pay twice as much for his supply of stale lager. That's what we are: not equal partners, nor employees, nor the geese that lay the golden eggs, but barrels of Carling Black Label, getting perilously near to our sell-by date.

So, here's the gruesome triple whammy for British opera singers: a dearth of work and financial support at home, even more so than before this latest shit-show; epidemiological pariah status abroad, with uncertainty over travel bans and two-week quarantines making it harder than ever to find work elsewhere; and a UK passport which is, for the foreseeable future, hardly worth the pretty blue paper it's printed on.

It's the perfect storm. And any British opera singer who survives it deserves every reward they get.

An artistic ecosystem where the artists are constantly pushed further and further towards the bottom of the food chain cannot possibly hope to thrive in the long term.

So I hope I'm wrong. I hope those now in a position to help us, those running the organisations which will receive large chunks of the £1.57bn – siphoned from our own past and future taxes – will take a wider view; and despite the narrow constraints of what our self-consuming industry requires of them, start to think of ways in which British opera singers – that huge native natural resource which they only occasionally have the courage, imagination and expertise to tap into – could be saved.

Otherwise this might be the moment that UK opera finally eats itself. Where buildings and offices are maintained while artistic talent is left to wither and die. Where all that remains is the imported husk of an irrelevant foreign museum piece, as our detractors so often sneeringly accuse us of being.

And if that's all we're capable of, none should mourn our passing.

6.7.2020

13. Who cares about composers?
1st August 2020

Hacker: Let us choose what we subsidise, by the extent of popular demand.
Sir Humphrey: What would happen to the Royal Opera House on such a basis? The very summit of our cultural achievement.
Hacker: And what do they do? Mozart, Wagner, Verdi, Puccini. Germans and Italians! It's not our culture at all.
- Yes Minister, Season 3 Episode 7: "The Middle-Class Rip-Off"

The lurching has begun. Yesterday, a couple of UK concert venues, brave enough to take a step towards re-opening under current government guidance, had to take at least one step back within hours as that guidance changed with minimal notice.

Meanwhile, one of the government's scientific advisors is today suggesting that pubs may have to close once schools reopen, in order to keep the infection rate under control. Follow the logic of this, if you haven't already. In terms of the complete certainty of preventing infection, pubs are not safe. Schools are not safe. Planes are not safe. And no, concert halls and theatres are not safe either. None of them are safe, in any country which has neglected to do the hard work of eliminating the virus from circulation entirely.

The judgement the government is currently making is about whose health and lives should be put on the line in return for keeping society functioning. It's worth bearing this in mind each time we call for our audiences to be allowed to return to their seats. Not to mention the next time we're in front of a ballot box: what kind of people do we want making these unenviable decisions on our behalf?

Having said that, politician-bashing is far too much of a comfort zone for artists. Any successful negotiation has to take account of the opposing side's world-view. It's something for which we readily criticise our leaders, regarding recent dealings with the European Union for example, and yet we're guilty of the same sin ourselves. If we genuinely want something from our political leaders, we need to make the effort to explain it to them in their terms, not ours.

The fact is that Jim Hacker's point is a fair one. It's not a conversation that would need to happen in Germany or Italy, or France or Russia for that matter; the intrinsic importance of their operas to their culture needs no explanation.

But British opera has this problem, and we hardly help ourselves. Sir Humphrey's beloved Royal Opera House staged a work by Benjamin Britten last year for only the second time since 2013, and even then only ventured to schedule five performances of *Death in Venice* – to rave reviews and packed houses. Hopefully a lesson was learned, because if London's biggest companies aren't brave enough to stick their necks out for Britten, then we really are in trouble.

Choose to be bold, and doors might open. German and Italian opera has a problem that we don't: undeniably, their greatest works are at least a hundred years old. That means that German and Italian opera houses are inevitably museums to some extent. That's an issue when it comes to presenting opera as a living, breathing art form, reflecting society today and responding to its needs. It's not an insurmountable problem, but it's one which we in Britain have chosen to make ours too, by relying so heavily on old, imported material.

Many regular opera-goers will be scratching their heads at the idea that contemporary composers and modern music could be the solution to the challenges we face. Let's be honest, most of them decided some time ago that they hate all that stuff. Even those that are willing to attend new opera often do so out of a sense of reluctant duty rather than any great thirst for the unfamiliar.

In many cases their lack of enthusiasm might have been justified. And that's largely our fault. Over the last century or so, the standard process of creating an opera has evolved to a state where you frequently get the distinct impression that we're more comfortable working with dead composers, since they're far less trouble.

But dead composers ultimately lead to a dead art form. Mozart, Wagner, Verdi and Puccini were all intimately involved in the creation of their works, not just from conception to written page, but right the way through to opening night and beyond. That way of doing it was clearly established as the best practice, leading to what are still viewed as the best results. But too often since then we've taken the soft option of keeping the composer out of the rehearsal room, and we've paid the price.

It's important to note the success stories too. The ROH's *Death in Venice* sold out. So did recent productions of John Adams' *Nixon in China* and Philip Glass's *Akhnaten* at English National Opera. Admittedly those are works which are now decades old, but the crucial point is that their composers found various ways of engaging with the public response to their music, and what purpose their work might serve, along with the opportunities to allow that input to feed back into their future work. New operas need several outings to hit home – too often they're discarded almost as soon as they're written, with no thought as to where they go next.

From my own experience, the creation of new operas is an infinitely more effective, not to mention personally rewarding, process when the composer is as close to the trial-and-error loop as possible, an open, active and equal partner from day one to dress rehearsal. It's not always easy – the soft option is to keep the number of egos in a rehearsal room to a minimum – but if composers are to have a chance of developing a sense of how to create operas that the public want to hear, it is life-or-death essential.

And it's something we can start right now, under current conditions. Companies have empty rehearsal facilities. The rest of us have time on our hands. Why not put a composer, a librettist, a pianist and a couple of singers in a room, give them a small budget and see what emerges?

This is the sort of thing we should be thinking about when we attempt to address the issues of how the industry distributes its crisis funds to its freelance artists. By the time we're out the other end, we might have something compelling to show for it.

More than that, we might have stories to tell. A lot of Britain's current problems stem from difficulties in relating to our own past, our historical and current relationship with our own culture and with other countries and their people. We're more comfortable with imported art because we shy away from engaging with our own stories. Perhaps it's time to face up to that. And because it's not a crowded field in terms of existing repertoire, British opera should be well-placed to play its part, given a brave enough vision on the part of its artistic leaders.

British music, British voices, British stories. There's your slogan right there. Even a politician could understand it.

1.8.2020

14. Counting the Peanuts
8th August 2020

Live classical performance is getting back on its feet, slowly. The "New Normal": smaller audiences, smaller programmes. And entirely unsurprisingly, and in most cases understandably, smaller fees for the performers. Tentative enquiries are trickling in, and most of them involve paying a fraction – by which I mean considerably less than half – of what the going rate was before.

Which is fine. We all want to get this thing back on its feet, and taking a short term financial hit to make that happen is something most singers will be willing to do, especially for employers who have shown them loyalty in the past.

Let's get some context here. Surely opera singers get paid megabucks, right? So most of them can stand to go without caviar and a new Rolex for six months or so.

Hmm. For comparison, if you wanted to book a commercial classical "crossover" singer to come and sing for twenty minutes at your product launch or birthday party, you'd have to stump up more money than I've ever earned in a year. And you wouldn't haggle, you'd find the money to pay the going rate or look elsewhere.

Many of these crossover singers are my friends, and I don't begrudge them a penny of what they earn – they provide a product, they've worked hard for it, and they deserve the rewards. The difference is that their employers are willing to find the funding for what they perceive as quality. They are right – whatever your views on their taste when it comes to singing – not least because it means that, if they want to book the same singer next year, that singer will still be in business.

For those of us who are still naïve enough to be committed to singing in actual operas, our fees are much lower than they were for previous generations – and I don't mean allowing for inflation either, I'm talking about the actual number of pounds and dollars. Audiences often complain that the standard of singing isn't what it was in the past. Whether that's true or not, the unarguable fact is that we're being asked to do the same thing on an annual budget that a singer of another era would have spent on after shave.

So any time anyone tries to claim that singers' fees are the problem in the opera world's business model, please feel free to give them a metaphorical slap. Outside a very, very small number of "A-listers" of varying quality, most of us were struggling to get by even before our entire industry shut down overnight – often without even considering honouring existing contracts, or in many cases bothering to inform us that they were being cancelled.

Let's assume that by "opera singer" we mean someone who is capable of performing roles in operas, and maintaining the highest professional standards of doing that over a period of years and decades. That's an expensive business, and requires constant financial investment. For quite some time now the industry which depends on those standards being maintained has been increasingly unwilling to fund what that actually costs.

Whatever opera's problems are, artists' fees being too high is not one of them.

8.8.2020

15. Sick Pay and Quarantine
20th August 2020

"I've got a mortgage, a wife and six kids, and George Bush has just devalued the dollar. I can't afford to be here."

From his expression, I guessed my colleague wasn't exaggerating. And that was before he ended up in hospital for opening night.

Let's talk about how freelance opera soloists are paid. In general, all the factors – the value of work put in during rehearsals, travel and accommodation expenses, the time and expenditure of learning and preparing a role, and so on – are rolled together and presented as an overall fee per performance.

There are more sophisticated models, where the remuneration is broken down into rehearsal fees, expense allowances etc, but they're generally at the lower end of the pay scale. Companies tend to prefer the simplicity of the inclusive per-show fee – as do agents, who can then take their slice of that larger gross figure.

(Sometimes these days a flat fee – related to the show fee – is also included for rehearsals, essentially in the hope that it might persuade the superstars in the cast to turn up before the dress rehearsal.)

Back in the days when singers earned the price of a small house for a cough and a spit, this all probably worked out fine. But as margins have got tighter – as a general rule, opera singers' pay has moved in antiphase with professional footballers' – the shortcomings have emerged.

For one thing, singers have to pay their expenses up front, and then may not get paid for weeks after opening night, meaning there's a cashflow issue of several months. Given a steady cycle of work, this is on the whole manageable. But like a particularly traumatic game of musical chairs, when the music suddenly stopped a few months ago, many singers were left with a crippling amount of non-refundable outgoings, with the income which was supposed to cover them disappearing in a magic contract-transcending puff of "force majeure".

Another idiosyncrasy of this system is that, in the case of illness, the decision as to whether a singer performs or cancels is almost always left in the hands of the singer themselves. They can decide to soldier on, in which case they get paid, or to go home to bed, in which case they don't. But in the former situation, opera companies don't give themselves any option other than going ahead with a sick singer aerosolling away in a cramped theatre.

We wait with bated breath for Declan Costello's report on singing-related transmission of SARS-CoV-2, which is published tomorrow. Many singers have already seized on his Twitter preview as being the silver bullet we've all been waiting for, although even this first glance raises as many questions as it answers. Even the best-case comeback will be halting and messy – what the science can do is help us to do it as sustainably and safely as possible for all involved.

That latter point will become more important as the reality of rehearsing hits us, especially as more evidence emerges of the specific long-term dangers of Covid-19 to professional singers – an issue which far too many of my colleagues, in their understandable desperation to get back to work, continue to overlook. But already the last few months have provided much food for thought about singers and contagious illnesses in rehearsal and performance situations.

My American colleague fell seriously ill just before the *sitzprobe* stage of rehearsals, and was still in hospital on opening night. He missed the second show as well, and by this point things must have been getting financially serious for him. It was a run of eight performances (not at all an atypical number, and longer than many runs), so he'd already lost 25% of his overall income for the four month project. Bear in mind that as well as travel and accommodation, he'd need to pay taxes, agents' commission, and currency exchange fees, before he even began to think about sending a few quid home to his family. Miss another show and he'd probably be facing an overall loss on the whole contract.

Understandably, therefore, when it came to the third performance, there he was on stage. That he managed to haul himself out of a hospital bed to get there was a testament to his character and determination. But it was a deeply uncomfortable experience performing opposite a colleague and friend, all the while not knowing whether he would make it to the end of the show in one piece – and I don't mean vocally. He looked like death. But he couldn't afford not to be there.

As it happened, that was a non-contagious illness. Imagine the added complication if his presence was also endangering the health of those around him. Or indeed, what if he was perfectly capable of performing his role, but could be infecting his colleagues – perhaps via asymptomatic transmission of some new virus?

The decision as to whether a singer should perform or not cannot be left solely in the hands of that singer, when financially they may have no option. It's reasonable that they be given first call – for one thing, you can understand why a company might be keen for there to be as much incentive as possible for their A-listers to show up in the first place. But once the singer has declared themselves willing and able to perform, the company must surely now, more than ever, give themselves the option of keeping the singer away from the rest of the cast and crew, at no financial cost to the singer themselves.

There are plenty of problems raised by the current crisis to which there are no straightforward solutions. And it's important that we keep asking those questions, even when it's not clear that there are any answers, exhausting as that often is. But here's a problem with a ready solution – a simple, low-cost change that can, and should, be made right away.

20.8.2020

16. Beyond the Costello Report
30th August 2020

PANDEMIC COULD BE OVER WITHIN TWO YEARS!

screamed the headline from BBC News, followed immediately by,

CORONAVIRUS WILL BE WITH US FOREVER!

Cue many baffled posts on social media – couldn't the BBC make its mind up? Presumably the posters must think that when they blow out their birthday candles, the phenomenon of fire is extinguished forever. The virus will outlive the pandemic.

Shoddy headlines and cack-handed government advice notwithstanding, sometimes you have to wonder if the ignorance is wilful. The music industry looks on with envy as sports events get back up and running. Why aren't we allowed to go back to work too, musicians ask, conveniently overlooking the amount of time, effort and money that sports have put into adapting their ways of operating. They haven't been "allowed" to go back to work so much as made a persuasive case about how they can do so with the minimum risk to their employees, and the smallest possible impact on wider public health.*

Ten days ago, ENT surgeon Declan Costello and his colleagues published a scientific report into the aerosol concentrations produced by various types of singing, as well as by speaking and breathing. You can read the full thing online, and it's very much worth a few minutes of your time, since it's fascinating stuff. Many performers seized on it immediately as a green light to get back on stage. In fact it's far from that, and as with any good

83

scientific report, it raises at least as many questions as it answers. That's how science works.

The results suggest that singing doesn't produce a significantly greater amount of aerosols than speaking at a similar volume. Singing is safe! – cried those for whom it was crucial to believe that singing is safe. That's not quite what it says, and the results demand closer inspection and further exploration, in particular for those of us whose job frequently involves being in poorly-ventilated rooms full of people singing very loudly indeed.

So it's a start. We've established that there's no need to live in specific fear of singing, so conclusions and strategies are transferable. What we need to look at is how we put what we know into practice for safe rehearsing and performing.

It would be helpful if we were more careful about distinguishing between the situation for performers (and those working alongside them) – which should be about ensuring a minimum-risk working environment – and audiences, where the question is far more about the impact on the broader spread of the virus.

For the latter, the recent study by Berlin's Charité hospital should be seized upon by the industry, suggesting quite plausibly as it does that classical music audiences, being generally inclined towards disciplined behaviour when it comes to moving around, singing along, shouting and so on, should be safe enough if universally masked, and given a bit of thought as to possible bottlenecks during ingress and egress. Our audiences are used to being asked not to applaud between movements, or at the end of entire acts in the case of Parsifal, so they'd surely take this in their stride. (In fact, ahead of the curve as always, audiences have

84

been refraining from cheering during my curtain calls for several years now.)

The possibility of a near-capacity auditorium sometime soon would be a genuine game-changer for theatres and concert halls, and gut instinct surely tells us that there's a way of doing this relatively sensibly and safely, especially compared to a crowd at a rock concert or football match. Or indeed in a pub.

In terms of performers' safety, we could do with seeing further detail from the World Health Organisation on the relative importance of heavier particles (where social distancing and hand-washing are crucial factors) and aerosol transmission (where masks and ventilation are the principal weapons). Assuming the former still play a role – and there's no reason to think they don't – we need to know, for example, whether singing and speaking at higher volumes increases the range of those particles, something which the Costello report by definition doesn't explore. That would then inform us, for example, how far singers need to stand back from the edge of the orchestra pit when all guns are blazing. Orchestral players don't as a rule appreciate having to put their well-being on the line at work, and they're absolutely right about that.

There's one truly shocking thing about the Costello report though: that this vital research has only just taken place, and even then we depended on the initiative and generosity of a group of medical professionals to get it done. If the honours system stood for anything, Declan and his colleagues should be nailed-on for gongs all round. But the fact that it took them to do it off their own bat is a shameful condemnation of our own industry's collective lethargy since the crisis hit. Why was this study not commissioned by any of the hundreds of performing arts organisations now relying on it as a crucial piece of evidence, months ago and with a far more extensive remit?

Let's not get stuck on the retrospective blame game for now, since the clock is ticking ever louder. Costello's work suggests strongly that there's no distinction between different styles of singing, nor indeed between singing and the spoken word. This means that every single branch of theatre – sung and spoken, commercial and subsidised – shares an urgent existential interest in examining this further. Most of the issues being equally crucial to all, our industry leaders need to bang their heads together, pool their resources, and get the science done. We hear from them almost daily of the billions of pounds the performing arts are worth to the economy. It would take a tiny fraction of that to commission the work needed to get us back up and running with a vengeance.

Initiative, co-operation, a small amount of investment; and huge potential dividends. If our artistic leaders didn't know where to start or who to ask, they do now. There are no longer any valid excuses. We need fewer buts, and more Costellos.

30.8.2020

PS The most eye-catching part of the report for me was lines 220-227, and the related data around the variations in aerosol generation between individuals. In brief, a few people emit more just from breathing than most do from singing or shouting. Given that scientists have been on the hunt for months for explanations as to how super-spreading occurs, this is surely worth looking at in far greater depth, as the report itself recommends.

PPS The flautist Kathryn Williams has very helpfully been in touch with a link to the global literature review on performance and Covid-19 she has carried out with Dr Jodie Underhill for the Incorporated Society of Musicians. It's updated to 21st August 2020, available online for free, and is very much worth looking up.

* Update October 2020: football fans are still banned from attending matches in the UK, prompting them to ask, "If theatres are safe, why not football grounds?"

17. British Voices, British Stories
17th September 2020

As part of a recent discussion on the question of "colour-blind" casting in *Hamilton*, the New York Times quoted the playwright August Wilson, an excerpt from his 1996 speech *The Ground On Which I Stand.*

Wilson's compelling analysis of the shortcomings of colour-blind casting – "(Black Americans) do not need colorblind casting; we need theatres" – makes disquieting reading for those of us in an opera world which has settled on the comfortable assertion that any singer can portray any character as a straightforward panacea for accusations of institutional racism.

Wilson's arguments are worth reading in full, as is the article by the poet Maya Phillips in which he was quoted: both are freely available online. As a middle-aged white man, my role in these issues is mainly to listen and learn rather than wade in with largely unqualified opinions for the sake of having them.

Having said that, there are particular challenges for opera in this field, and they're mostly a result of our reliance on a core repertoire which is well over a hundred years old. A contemporary diversity of narrative voices is only possible, even in theory, if the material being produced is also contemporary. Colour-blind casting may limit the ability of stories to discuss historical questions of race (as Phillips asserts about *Hamilton*), but in opera's case those discussions, if they exist at all, are founded on a perspective which is centuries out of date.

In his article on classical music and race in this week's New Yorker, the critic and author Alex Ross asserts that

"Classical music can overcome the shadows of its past only if it commits more strongly to the present."

But there's an obvious problem here, and it's this: almost all the best operas were written by white European men between 1780 and 1920.

Most of them were German or Italian. Some of them were French or Russian. A few may have been homosexual. That's about as far as the diversity goes. You may choose to quibble according to your own personal taste – but if we define "best" as "those that the greatest number of people want to hear", then the case is pretty much closed. We've spent most of this year arguing about how, or whether, to define Beethoven's "greatness", and it's a fascinating discussion: but the bottom line is that lots of people really like listening to his music. (The proof surely being that no-one ever seriously argues that he's a "great" operatic composer, since *Fidelio* is hard work for even the most ardent listener.)

It's right that we examine our use of the concept of "greatness" as applied to composers, and even if we decide it's valid, whether basing it mostly on large-scale works is in itself exclusionary. But short of the invention of time travel, there are only so many non-white, non-male composers of these sorts of works that we can unearth historically. You can't rediscover what doesn't, what was denied the opportunity to, exist.

So where does that leave us? If I were German or Italian and writing this article, I'd probably end it here. It's not at all clear that the world needs any more German or Italian operas, although I'd be very happy to be convinced otherwise. Singers from other countries can look on with envy at how fundamentally those operas underpin the culture of their respective nations, and more than that, encapsulate their native relationship to language, emotion, and national character. Not that there isn't always something new to discover about those concepts, but in all honesty, they've got plenty to be getting on with, and I don't envy any contemporary composer trying to slot into that somewhere.

The British situation is different – it's hard to deny there's a gap in the market, since even the best-known British operas are hardly core repertoire worldwide, nor indeed even at home. The time is surely ripe for investing to change that. British opera companies are largely still in lockdown, their well-funded facilities lying unused behind locked doors. The idiosyncrasies of the UK's furlough payments have arguably meant that has had to be the case up till now, but as administrative staff get back to work, surely there's an opportunity to make use of practice rooms and rehearsal spaces, for composers and librettists to get together with singers and repetiteurs, and see what comes out. Any state-subsidised opera company needs to have some opera to show for their funding, or stands on precariously thin ice in political terms.

If now is not the time for British opera to pick itself up and allow itself to tell its own stories, then when will it ever be? And if British opera is truly concerned about problems of diversity, why should we continue to import many of those problems – from abroad, and from the past?

When I mentioned this idea – British music, British voices, British stories – at the end of my recent post on how opera has treated its composers in recent times, it provoked something of a backlash. That the idea of looking to native resources to produce work that is rooted in, reflects the state of, and has a chance of

91

speaking to contemporary society in Britain is often automatically assumed to be a narrow-minded, insular, exclusionary statement shows how far the task of defining nationalism has been surrendered by those who have a more outward-looking, inclusive view of it.

Make no mistake, it would be far more comfortable for our opera industry to continue to view ourselves as part of a broader pan-European tradition, to argue that the works of Wagner and Verdi and Bizet and Tchaikovsky course instinctively through the veins as the birthright of anyone who lives here.

But the problem is that we're not bringing anything much to the party ourselves. The recent, largely manufactured, controversy over the Last Night of the Proms at least showed that most Brits have an awareness of the tune and words of *Rule, Britannia!* and a vague understanding (or misunderstanding) of their meaning. Where is the operatic equivalent?

It's easy to complain about British opera companies importing singers for their limited performances right now, and it's certainly a legitimate point when so many British singers, whose taxes subsidise those same companies, are sitting at home at severe risk of going out of business. But those casting choices reveal the truth, if there was ever any doubt, that the British view opera as an exotic foreign art form, best performed by foreign singers if it's the real thing, and the British version as inferior fare. That this view clearly pervades even in parts of the very top of the British operatic establishment should serve as a wake-up call.

Opera puts words to music, and at its best turns those base elements into stories which speak in the most direct way to those for whom those words are an everyday language. If we truly care about accessibility, it starts right there. And in a modern world where, with few exceptions, operas are performed in their original language, that means producing new operas, now, in our own languages.

Furthermore, the absence of any great historical canon gives British opera a golden opportunity to address all those accusations of racism and misogyny. Opera uniquely gives voice to its characters in the most literal sense, in a way that other art forms can't. Relative to the prevailing sentiments of their era, Bizet's Carmen, Verdi's Violetta, Tchaikovsky's Tatyana are the dramatically-empowered protagonists of their stories to a degree that their literary counterparts could never be. Opera has the intrinsic power to tell the stories of contemporary Britain, from the perspective of those who live here now, if we choose to embrace the opportunity.

These are honest conversations which Britain desperately needs to have with itself. Few of us would have chosen to live in an era of toxic culture wars, but as artists we don't legitimately have the option in the long run of ignoring it, nor of planting ourselves on one side and sniping uncomprehendingly at the other, without ultimately making ourselves irrelevant. It's clear that the stories Britain tells itself, about itself, increasingly fail to make sense in the context of the modern world. We can help with that, if we're brave enough to tackle it. That's what stories are for, and stories are what we do.

Neither should we be afraid to acknowledge and embrace the diverse nature of historical British culture. Opera also deals with the fundamental relationship of a culture with emotion – hence German and Italian opera, for example, being very different from each other. As the child of a Welsh and Irish family, who's

93

lived large parts of his adult life in England and Scotland, it seems to me there's a stark variance in that relationship across the UK's constituent nations. Welsh opera, in both of its primary languages, has been largely neglected in recent decades, and the time must surely soon come when that is rectified on a national level. How about a Welsh operatic *Mabinogion*, *Dic Penderyn* or *Tryweryn*? An honest English examination of the Empire from the diverse perspectives of all involved? Hell, how about a Scottish *Macbeth*? Give voices a place on their own stage and they will tell their own stories.

British singers are among the most well-trained and versatile in the world – the huge numbers of youngsters who come to our music colleges and training schemes from across the globe is clear evidence of that. Look among their ranks and you will find examples of British and British-trained artists who can perform in German, Italian, French, Russian, Czech repertoire as authentically as most natives. May that never change, and may we continue to embrace the wider world, and be embraced by it. That we need simultaneously to find ways of breaking down the increasing social and financial barriers which stand in the way of nurturing operatic talent from all parts of British society is beyond question.

But at the same time, this fundamental British talent – in all its modern diversity – could also be given the chance to engage far more deeply with its own language, history, culture, challenges and opportunities. In other words, with its own stories. So that when our audiences are finally allowed to return, we have something new to tell them – something that speaks directly to them as modern Britons. The opera industry looks with scornful envy at its "crossover" rivals, at how the relatability of their stars with their recognisable back stories invites new audiences in a way that mainstream classical music can only dream of. And yet British opera so often fails to heed the clear lesson when it comes to employing and promoting the talent on its own doorstep.

It might well be the start of a long journey. We'd need to embrace our composers and decide to put them at the heart of the creative process from beginning to end. But our current catastrophic situation could be the chance to sow the seeds of the first real golden era of British opera. All it needs is a small amount of investment, vision and bravery from our artistic leaders.

Britain's singers are here, her composers and librettists are here; they're ready, and they've got stories to tell.

Let's give them the chance to tell those stories.

17.9.2020

18. No Longer Viable
26th September 2020

I check my bank balance. I have to do this on an ATM because it's 1998: the 24th of September, which was a Thursday. I know that for a fact, because pay day was always the last Thursday of the month. But this isn't a pay day for me. It's the first one I've missed.

I'd been working as a secondary school Physics teacher – in effect a job for life, with excellent prospects given the scarcity of graduates in the subject, especially in the Welsh language sector. But the lure of seeing where my singing hobby could take me if I applied myself to it full-time was too seductive to resist. It isn't until that first missing paycheque that the reality of the leap I've taken hits home.

What have I done?

Last Thursday, as coincidence would have it the 24th of September 2020, the Chancellor of the Exchequer announced his latest scheme for supporting the UK economy through the next stages of the continuing crisis, which, he explained, "means supporting people to be in viable jobs". In a contrast to previous Rishi-grams, the reaction from most of my self-employed colleagues was underwhelming, to say the least. Later that day the Conservative MP Anthony Browne told BBC Radio 4 that "I advise all musicians to get another job. There are many expanding sectors with job availability".

Staring down the other end of a barrel which is precisely 22 years long. In a television interview about singing as a career I gave while still a student, I was asked where I saw myself in twenty years' time.

97

"Anywhere except on the dole", flippant smart-arse twenty-something me answered. The quip has come back to haunt his middle-aged counterpart over the last six months.

If it was still unclear to anyone in the UK performing arts that this is going to be a long, hard struggle, with no guarantee of there being anything much left at the end of it, the penny must surely have dropped this last week. Wednesday's announcement that the Metropolitan Opera in New York would remain closed until September 2021 at the earliest sent shock waves through the industry. The Met is the top of the food chain. Maybe it makes sense that the largest carnivores would find it hardest to dodge the meteorite, but the emotional crater was nonetheless huge.

Meanwhile, surely the smaller, more agile omnivores and herbivores should be better suited to survive? The accurate description of evolution is survival of the most adaptable, rather than the fittest, after all.

The problem with that analogy is that we're facing the wiping out of an entire ecosystem, rather than the ultimately necessary culling of one or two weaker or obsolete species within it. Being a professional musician is a full-time job, even if the bit of it that looks like "work" is sporadic. There's a delicate virtuous circle of performance, study, rest and practice that in the long run can't be reconciled with the distraction of a second, unrelated career. There's really no such thing as a "semi-professonal" musician, only amateurs and pros, and the distinction is not one of talent or knowledge or ability, but one of time and commitment. Once you disrupt that balance and interrupt the cycle, it becomes increasingly difficult to get it back.

In other words, if we send our musicians away to other jobs, most of them will not be returning. The leap into the precarious career of an artist is terrifying, and not one which most people would make at all, let alone twice. So once what we have in this country – our vast reservoir of immensely skilled artistic talent – is gone, it will be gone for good.

What can we do? Anger, criticism and lobbying has thus far been directed at the government and MPs. That's a good starting point and, in a concrete and focused way, needs to continue; but taking on board three hard realities. Wider public support is mixed and lukewarm. Mr Browne's attitude is probably quite typical of the modern breed of Tory – these are politicians who would take being labelled ultra-Darwinist as a compliment. And the government clearly feels it's already done more than enough to help the arts.

Whether they're right or wrong about the last point, it does raise the question of how the industry intends to help itself – in other words, what are the arts going to do to help artists? Brave pioneering and innovative one-off opera productions are a huge morale-booster, but ultimately the performing model needs to get back to something sustainable – near-capacity audiences on a wide scale – for the freelance operatic ecosystem to survive to any extent. Performances in Paris and other European cities are being held along what seem almost-normal lines, with a little social distancing, compulsory mask-wearing and so on. Surely the UK government can be persuaded to allow something similar; and, at the risk of turning into some sort of aerosolic Cato the Elder, surely the industry can make its case far more persuasive by funding some basic research into how safe it would be?

Opera companies must also think about how they can launch some lifeboats. Even in the face of prospective job losses, they should contemplate how at least a few artistic careers might be saved by moving away from the obsolete brutality of a pure freelance system. What good is an arts industry without artists? Put a few freelancers on contract, even if only for the short term and on minimal wages, and they just might still be artists on the other side of this – and could provide some sorely-needed creative input in the meantime. Not all souls could be saved this way, but that's no excuse for letting the whole crew drown.

The hardest hit by all of this are the young artists just starting out in their careers. If this is the end of the world as we know it, at least old lags like me have had our moment in the sun, however truncated. Young singers are being kneecapped before they've had any time to get going. During their training they'll have been told to build up a contingency fund – it's fair to say that very few people saw a pandemic coming, but singers lose voices, break limbs and so on, so a rainy-day back-up of a few months' income is always judicious. But it takes a few years to build that up, and they haven't had a chance.

Most of them will not want to follow the official advice and get another job, but many will have no alternative. The problem is that an alternative career, even as a contingency plan, makes its own immediate demands on your time and energy. A young singer might see this now as clearly a short-term stopgap. But as the months and perhaps years drag on, the ex-singer makes progress in their new career – our youngsters are generally a bright and versatile lot, and most would be an asset to any line of work – and they contemplate a return to an industry which is still struggling to revive itself, with singers paid less and singing given less of a priority even than before, that sense of clarity might fade.

What then for an industry model which has evolved to depend on a steady supply of (cheap) young talent? Where then for music colleges which have depended on being able to persuade young people that a viable career exists for them in a thriving classical music industry? Those singers with wealthy family or friends might make it through, but are we really content to stand idle and lose our traditional wealth of talent from less privileged, more diverse backgrounds? No one could blame any young artist for jumping ship right now, and no one who leaves the profession in 2020 should do so tinged with any sort of sense of failure: the failure is the industry's, not theirs. And the loss would ultimately be ours, not theirs.

Once what we had is gone, it will be gone for good. This crisis is not going away. We need to think seriously about what we want to be left with at the end of it.

26.9.2020

19. Carthago delenda est
2nd October 2020

"Be prepared to say goodbye to movie theaters."

The Washington Post's headline struck me as a little click-baity, but I bit anyway. What happened next did, for once, shock me.

Megan McArdle's opinion piece from last Sunday (28th September) is quietly but strongly argued, and makes sobering reading for anyone who loves cinema. It's even stronger medicine for anyone involved in the far less profitable branches of the dramatic and musical arts.

The article points out that Hollywood has so far tried two approaches to the challenges of launching new movies in lockdown: one-off monetised streaming (Disney's latest live-action version of *Mulan*), and longer runs in reduced-capacity auditoriums (Christopher Nolan's delightfully baffling *Tenet*). The industry's response to the results of these kite-flying experiments has been to push every other major cinematic release back into 2021.

In other words, both approaches have failed. All that's left is for them to sit tight and hope they can get back to their old full-capacity-multiplex-based business model before the whole industry goes bust.

If even Hollywood is struggling to find a way to make this work, then we really are in trouble. In the blog that kicked off this series, I made the point that the streaming services run by Disney and company are revenue-generating and, at least in principle, financially viable. Classical music, meanwhile, was splurging all its content online, for free, forever. We were, and remain, so far behind them that the idea digital content could somehow ride to our rescue was always far-fetched. In the light of clear evidence that even Hollywood can't get it to pay its own way, our naivety seems laughable.

Those multiplexes form a cinematic ecosystem – a Great Barrier Reef for the blockbuster movie industry. What the evidence seems to show is that you can't drastically reduce its food supply and expect the reef to survive. And while you could always artificially recreate a small part of it at an aquarium, in concrete rather than coral, it's hardly the same thing.

As the dust settles on the Metropolitan Opera's announcement of cryogenic storage till September 2021, the most disturbing aspect of it is that you worry deep down that, at least in brutal economic terms, they may be right. Perhaps opera in a time of Covid is like a hard border in Northern Ireland and there really is no miraculous modern solution to making it work, however clever and innovative we are.

At the very least, Hollywood's struggles imply strongly that digital content for classical music would require a custom-built business model if it were ever to break even – note Disney's decision to delay the release of (stand-alone movie) B*lack Widow* and instead make *Wandavision* (a subscription channel TV series) the launchpad for Phase 4 of the Marvel Cinematic Universe. Online content needs to be purpose-built.

Indigo's most recent survey on attitudes to the performing arts online provides some glimpses of hope for our industry: for instance, 79% of opera fans stated that they were keen to engage with digital content, the highest score of any art form. Opera's audiences are a constant source of pleasant surprises, and are one of the main reasons to be optimistic for our future. But the question of whether classical music's digital content can ever break even, and if so how we get to that point, remains a deeply problematic one.

Whichever way you look at it, the inescapable truth is that in the short term, the UK opera industry will only really survive this crisis in anything like its current form if we can get back to performing to near-capacity audiences as soon as possible. That is the "viable" version of the industry. I suggest that requires a two-pronged approach, one political and one scientific.

Science first, since I've discussed this prong several times before. We need to find a way of showing that near full capacity audiences in theatres can be achieved without posing a serious health risk to those present and to the wider population. Public Health England have just, at long last, updated their advice to confirm that SARS-CoV-2 spreads via airborne transmission. That means that, given mask-wearing and other behavioural adaptations, plus good ventilation, a less extreme approach to social distancing might be possible – hence fuller auditoriums.

But the industry needs to be willing to help itself and give those in authority the confidence to make these decisions. We should be funding some simple but rigorous studies to model aerosol spread in the setting of a typical theatre auditorium – driving our scientific understanding forward rather than just following that which already exists.

Since this would benefit pretty much every branch of theatre, you might hope that some pooling of resources would be possible. However, there's a suspicion that the moguls of commercial theatre, however much they protest otherwise, might well prefer to keep their venues shut for the time being, taking the opportunity to make redundancies, replace expensive classic productions with new, cheaper versions (cheaper for them, that is – don't expect ticket prices to fall), and other such profit-enhancing tricks.

So be it; capitalists gonna capitalist. That leaves the subsidised branches of the industry to take up the slack and bear the burden – there should still be plenty of them to chip in. Reliable scientific studies would also address the concerns of the 86% of audience members in that Indigo survey who stated that they'd require some manner of additional reassurance before returning confidently to theatres and concert halls.

On the political side, while it's tempting to bash the government for not making the performing arts their highest priority in the process of opening the country back up, we need to accept that it's highly unlikely their world-view on that is going to change anytime soon. (It seems 86% of our audience would need more than just the government's word for it anyway.) The trick with politicians is to engage them on their territory, not yours. Preaching about how much we love and miss our jobs may be charming but doesn't really cut much ice with our hard-nosed elected leaders.

So the point that needs to be emphasised in this context is the value, direct and indirect, of the arts to the economy, and the irrefutable logic that the economy will therefore need the creative industries to be in a position to hit the ground running as soon as we're given the green light. That means a bit of help from the Treasury now, so that we can pay it back with interest as soon as they're ready to let us get cracking.

Ed Miliband, defying expectations by showing the value of experienced politicians remaining in their careers even after electoral failure, rather than going off and taking a quick buck of memoirs and after-dinner speeches (the arts aren't the only field struggling with talent retention at the moment), made a persuasive case in the Commons on Tuesday: these are not "unviable" jobs, but perfectly viable industries which have shut down for the greater public good, and therefore need and deserve support until that decision is reversed. That's a solid argument and the correct approach.

In other words, we now need to look to the other side of this river we find ourselves crossing, with greater clarity about the spot we're heading for, along with stronger evidence that it will be safe dry land, and a more focused approach to lobbying our leaders for specific forms of help in bridging the gap.

We're now past the six month mark in this global crisis, and it seems a lot of friends and colleagues have been finding it a tough milestone, especially when it feels in many ways that we're right back where we started. Seeing a limited number of live events get up and running almost makes it harder for those performers who aren't involved, since the idea that we were all in the same boat was at least some sort of comfort. The human cost of this pandemic, in lives, and in physical and emotional health, has been incalculable.

But we are moving forward, and progress is being made, even if it doesn't feel like it. If we can keep connecting with each other, keep allowing ourselves the time to take on board what has been lost, and then energise ourselves to move forward in a direction we choose, we can and will get through this.

Good luck, and don't stop hoping.

2.10.2020

20. Sculptures in Air
9th October 2020

In 1631, Count John Maurice of Nassau-Siegen bought a plot of land bordering the Binnenhof and the adjacent Hofvijver pond in The Hague. Five years later he was appointed Governor of Dutch Brazil, and while he was away, on that plot of land he had a house built, which is now known as the *Mauritshuis*.

John Maurice's house is filled these days with nearly 800 paintings, and the best of them is saved till last. By the time you meet Johannes Vermeer's *Meisje met de parel*, you've waded through several large floors of several hundred portraits. And yet she immediately demands your attention, turning your head towards her as soon as you enter the room like a diminutive but intensely powerful magnet. Beguiling and irresistible, once you've met her, you never forget her.

The Royal Opera House has just taken the unenviable decision to sell one of its own collection of artworks, a portrait by David Hockney of their former Chief Executive, Sir David Webster, hoping to raise as much as £18m at auction to help keep the company afloat. I must have walked past the painting many times, and with no disrespect to artist or subject, it's no Pearl Earring: I can't recall ever having given *Kerel zittend in een stoel met wat tulpen* so much as a second glance.

Webster was at the heart of the creation of Covent Garden as we know it today, so a public recognition of his significance is entirely appropriate – and since the Hockney portrait was the result of a staff whip-round, there's clearly a great deal of sentimental value attached too. But ultimately it's an opera house, not an art gallery. Selling off Callas' iconic red dress from *Tosca* might be a different matter, but if losing one painting means gaining several more operas, then it's clearly the right decision.

And also, blimey, eighteen million quid? That buys you a *lot* of opera. Somehow we don't question that contrast, even though the portrait is essentially the work of one artist, whereas any opera is the combination of dozens, if not hundreds. Aha, you say, but once you buy the painting you have it forever, whereas an opera is something you're obliged to share, and is gone as soon as it's over.

"Art is how we decorate space; music is how we decorate time." – Jean-Michel Basquiat

My favourite moment in opera comes at the start of Act 1 of Verdi's *Simon Boccanegra*. We've sat through a Prologue of men singing about serious man things. And then we hear a woman's solo voice for the first time that evening – Amelia Grimaldi, Boccanegra's long-lost daughter, singing of the beauty of the dawn and her grief at the death of her mother. Towards the end of the aria, she is answered by a three note figure from an oboe, which is the most beautiful thing Verdi ever wrote. A lesser composer would have flogged it to death throughout the rest of the opera; Verdi, having pricked our ears, gives us one more fleeting glimpse of it, and then eschews it forever after, leaving us only with the achingly bittersweet memory of how it made us feel at that moment.*

When I'm teaching singers, if they're trying too hard to push the sound into a big hall, one of the things I try to emphasise is that all we can ever do as musicians is to vibrate the molecules around us, and let the air in the room do the rest. We are sculptors of air, and air being a gas, those sculptures are necessarily short-lived; in

110

fact, that's part of their beauty. It's our mortality that makes life so precious.

That's why the feeling of holding your first album in your hands – the physical copy, with artwork and literature, rather than just the audio tracks – is a very different experience for a singer. At last, you've created something permanent, something that will last – something that, in a few years' time at least, when the memory of the sweat and tears which went into making it has faded and you can ignore its remaining imperfections, you might actually be able to sit down and enjoy yourself.

Wexford, 2005. We were performing a new production of Fauré's *Pénélope***, and between rehearsals I was busy preparing my first professional videos, and had uploaded a couple to the then new-fangled YouTube. My wise colleague Gerard Powers, having made the obligatory complimentary noises, then sounded a note of caution: be prepared to delete them at some point fairly soon; bear in mind that you'll be compared directly with whoever is up next on the playlist. My current repertoire being what it is, these days that usually ends up being George London or prime era Dietrich Fischer-Dieskau, which seems especially unfair. I guess Gerry had a point.

Those involved in auditioning singers are currently looking at ways of standardising recording technology – implicitly (and sometimes explicitly) acknowledging that modern recordings are not to be trusted. Pictures are photoshopped; audio tracks are sonically airbrushed in a similar way. There's an honest and dishonest version of each process: the aim of the morally acceptable version is to produce something which is *more* like the real-life entity than a two-dimensional photo, or a limited audio recording, could

111

otherwise achieve. (At the end of the day, if the other path is taken, the impressive effect only lasts until you meet the subject in the flesh – so it can only take you so far, and in a questionable direction at that.)

The goal of most recording engineers over the last couple of decades has been to reproduce the organic sound by creating as sterile an environment for the actual recording as possible. Understandably, something different is required for auditions – the results I've seen and heard so far of this new virtual format are interesting, and you can see why they might be more use for audition panels. What they don't lend themselves to is repeated listening – by the standards of modern recordings, they are raw and harsh on the ear – hence our quest for a smoother flawlessness in commercial recordings. And it's also why some modern audience members struggle with live performances, if they're expecting the glossy perfection they're used to from their CDs at home. They miss the point that perfect is easy enough; fabulous is something much harder.

"It's not the note you play that's the wrong note – it's the note you play afterwards that makes it right or wrong." – Miles Davis

The other thing I remind singing students of a lot is that you can't fix a note once you've sung it, only accept it and use it to move on to something more beautiful. As a singer you can never hear your own voice anyway – no, not even on a recording – so we are, uniquely as musicians, entirely reliant on the ears of others to tell us whether we're sounding good or not. That's why we have to be very careful about whose ears we choose to trust. Listening is very subjective, and so if we seem rude in dismissing your opinion of what you just heard, with apologies I'm afraid it comes with the job.

Whatever the song was has already dissipated, and who's to say categorically whether it was a thing of beauty or not?

Perhaps some note of caution about selling the family silver to fund opera is in order – you might argue that the opulence of the surroundings is an intrinsic part of the experience of a visit to Covent Garden. We should definitely be wary, in the quest to make it happen at all, of diluting the experience of a night at the opera to the point where people don't see the point of coming back, or of taking the risk in the first place in these uncertain times.

The exchange of the permanent charms of paint on canvas for the fleeting grace of a sculpture in air might make no long-term sense in bald economic terms. But for an opera house, under the current circumstances, it is surely the correct choice. Wherever the portrait of David Webster ends up, it will probably get more attention than it used to. And if a glimpse of a painting is the highlight of your evening in the theatre, then those of us on stage aren't doing our jobs.

9.10.2020

* Simon Boccanegra is Verdi's greatest composition, and is ruined only by people occasionally deciding to perform it.

** Pénélope is Fauré's greatest composition, and is ruined only by people never deciding to perform it.

Update October 2020: the Hockney portrait sold at auction for £12.8m. Still a lot of opera.

21. Local Heroes
23rd October 2020

In the autumn of 1933, Adolph Arthur "Harpo" Marx crossed the Atlantic by boat and traversed Europe by train, on a journey which would culminate in him being the first American to perform in the Soviet Union.

Despite some initial culture clashes and typically Marxian/Marxist confusions, Harpo's six week tour was a triumph. This was in no small part down to the moment where, once the Moscow hierarchy had correctly gauged his cultural importance, Harpo was presented with a full Russian team of producer, director, assistant producer, musical director, two writers, arranger, stage manager, company manager, scenic director, assistant director, plus a full cast of players to learn the roles usually played by the other Marx Brothers, and adapt them for the conventions of the local audience.

Marx's autobiography, which could only ever have been titled *Harpo Speaks*, is endlessly fascinating, in particular his description of growing up in a New York we can barely believe existed so recently. It's a small world too: Chico's first performing job turns out to be as a replacement for the previous teenage pianist at a nickelodeon cinema, who had been fired "because customers complained his music hurt their ears". His name was George Gershwin.

Seventy six years after Harpo's Russian triumph. Scottish Opera staff producer Robert Jones is standing in the wings of the Mariinsky Theatre in St Petersburg. Anna Netrebko has recently had her first child, and Valery Gergiev has told her to name the date and role for her return to the stage. She picks *Lucia di*

Lammermoor, and the most suitable production currently available has been shipped over from Glasgow, revival director and all. (Whether Robert travelled in one of the shipping containers is unclear, but I wouldn't have put it past him.)

Rehearsals are in full swing, although Netrebko has yet to appear, her able deputy filling in for her in the meantime. Robert turns around in the dark to find a young woman sitting in front of him, dressed in what is unmistakably Lucia's costume – but she is neither Netrebko nor her alternate. He introduces himself, and politely enquires who she might be. "I am D-cast Lucia." No fewer than four Lucias, with a spare always on hand ready to go at a moment's notice.

To our modern Western eyes, both situations seem like unbelievable extravagances. And surely, for us, unnecessary ones? Our opera companies often operate without understudies at all, since we can fly replacements in at a few hours' notice. And similarly, these days surely the full troupe of Marx Brothers and support team would fly in to Moscow, set up, do their stuff, and fly straight out again.

When the current pandemic hit, I was just finishing an article on the challenges of Brexit for British freelance musicians. And before that, I was working on a piece about climate change and the classical music business. The common theme in all three crises is that of an industry addicted to fast, cheap international travel.

We're hardly alone in that, of course. Across the globe, airlines are propped up by taxpayers' money, dropping prices far below their real cost to humanity, and millions of individual financial decisions are made on a false premise. The whole "if a crowded aeroplane is safe, why isn't a theatre?" argument misses the point that airlines have to be saved and kept running, since we seem incapable of imagining a way of life without air travel on tap whenever and wherever we want it. The recent "flights to nowhere" - trips of up to three hours which start and end in the same airport - are only the most absurd example of that, like undergoing unnecessary root canal surgery for the fun of it.

British orchestras are, like most musical organisations, struggling under the current circumstances. In a way this might seem odd, since a half-capacity (and therefore socially-distanceable) audience is a far from uncommon sight in London's concert halls. But what's missing from that equation are the well-funded foreign dates in the same tour which would absorb the losses of the UK performances – in other words, our orchestras and concert venues are effectively subsidised by other countries. Covid or not, that system was always going to have to adapt to the challenges of Brexit; and Brexit or not, the challenges of climate change.

Whichever way you look at it, the classical music industry needs to wean itself off its addiction to unsustainably cheap air travel.

What might that look like? Those old Soviet and Russian systems provide at least a hint of evidence that an alternative is possible, although it need not be anywhere near as financially extravagant. I cite those examples only as a nudge to those my age and younger in this part of the world, who have no recollection of the time before our current way of doing things, with its versatility, variety, and attendant precariousness.

Aside from his music, one of the main reasons we're spending a whole year venerating Beethoven is surely his significance in establishing the idea of musicians as independent artists, rather than servants and travelling salesmen, getting paid only for flogging their latest product. As singers, in lapsing back into an entirely freelance way of life, we've allowed ourselves to let a large part of Beethoven's greatest achievement slip through our fingers.

Ours is a brutally efficient system – and, as the last few months have surely proved beyond any doubt, the flip side of efficiency is fragility. Consider the starkly differing fortunes of singers based in the USA, with its Darwinistic capitalist approach, and Germany, with its less efficient but far more robust system. There are uncertain times ahead, and further global crises to come. Now is surely the time to consider ways of bolstering the fragility, even if it means sacrificing a degree of efficiency.

For this to happen, the opera industry is going to need to overcome its fear of singers.

It may seem strange to think of anyone involved in opera as being cantorphobic, but the industry as a whole is as a rule shockingly bad at plucking up the courage to ask singers what they think. And each new step towards greater efficiency has usually also involved a step away from putting singing at the core of what opera is about.

Why might that be? Well, the human voice is a sensitive and capricious beast, and requires careful handling. And just as only a jockey can really understand a thoroughbred racehorse, only a singer can truly know what a voice needs to perform the extreme tasks that opera demands of it.

Singers have a reputation for *being difficult*, and whatever the truth of that historically, in the vast majority of cases these days that reputation is completely unfounded. Using the human voice as a professional musical instrument is indeed difficult, and if an operatic production is conceived without any thought as to whether it might help or hinder the singing, you can probably expect the singers to raise objections; just as you might well expect a jockey to raise objections to flogging a racehorse to death through a lack of care and understanding on the part of its owners and trainers. Anyone who views that as *being difficult* doesn't truly have the best interests of opera at heart.

The decreasing presence of singers on the permanent staff of opera companies - in many cases, they're now absent altogether - causes an unhealthy imbalance in the knowledge and priorities of those companies. Even those members of staff keen to understand more about singing have nowhere to turn if there are no singers in the building as a matter of daily routine to provide their point of view. That's not to devalue the importance of those in administrative or other artistic roles - opera is the ultimate team effort, and each has their crucial part to play. But surely it shouldn't be controversial to say that singers, too, are a vital cog in the machine.

Because in the long run, if opera isn't about singing, it's about nothing. Yes, yes, it's the ultimate collaborative art form, we all get that. But you can see sets and costumes as beautiful, theatres as impressive, performers as dramatically engaging elsewhere. Hell, you can even hear music every bit as good. And if any of those elements is missing in opera, it often fails to satisfy fully. But if the singing isn't as good as it possibly can be, and needs to be, then none of the other parts can possibly make up the shortfall of the whole.

And if opera has to have singing at its very core to succeed, that too is where the singers must be. Let's be realistic here - I know we're not heading back to an era of expensive and cumbersome full teams of company principals any day soon, in this country at least. Although having said that, since the first couple of weeks rehearsing with any ad hoc cast is largely spent getting to know each other, a regular corps of artists who are familiar with their way of working saves wise companies time, and therefore money. And one way or another, major opera companies, whose funding and administration operates on a year-round basis, risk their very existence if they don't strive to provide year-round opera.

The step away from a non-disposable approach to singers is one down a slippery slope, where companies open themselves up to the temptation of producing anything other than opera - which, let's face it, is almost always the easier and more profitable option.

As the combined effect of current and coming crises causes the world to get larger again, opera companies need to re-engage with the communities from which they first sprung. Audiences and critics may need weaning off the assumption that the lure of the foreign and exotic is automatically superior to the home-grown product, but that can be a positive thing, if the opportunity is seized, and needn't mean entirely excluding guest artists from abroad either. I always find it easier to adapt my work to a new part of the world when I'm alongside colleagues familiar with how things work there. Even the genius of Harpo needed local help to make the Soviet Union laugh.

The opera industry needs to find better ways of listening to its singers, and of embracing them into its decision-making processes, from the most mundane to the highest, long-term strategic level. Not that opera companies should be run for the benefit of their singers; but maximising the quality of their singing should be at the core of every move a company makes. It won't necessarily make anyone's life easier. But it'll make the singing better.

And, dare I say it, that's what opera is about.

23.10.2020

22. The New Normal
24th October 2020

"A new scientific truth does not triumph by convincing its opponents and making them see the light, but rather because its opponents eventually die, and a new generation grows up that is familiar with it."
- Max Planck, Scientific Autobiography and Other Papers

It's six months to the day since I started on this journal in earnest. Much has changed since then, although in many ways it also feels like we're back to square one, with the government umm-ing and ahh-ing over the need for a second lockdown, in the face of a seemingly inexorable second wave of the virus.

The classical music world is grinding asymmetrically back into some sort of life. German-style systems across Europe appear to be coping better than most, their inherent robustness serving them well. Employing permanent teams of opera singers is a great incentive towards finding them something to do. In the United States, the entire industry seems to have been placed in cryogenic storage until some point next year, and the devil take the hindmost, which in practice largely means the artists. The UK, as usual, falls somewhere between those two extremes.

My forecast back in April of this crisis lasting well into 2021 if not beyond still looks fairly solid, and was based on a small degree of scientific insight. A vaccine by November was always a large slice of politically convenient optimism, and it's important for us to realise that unlike in Hollywood movies, an effective vaccine won't instantly solve all of our problems - like getting married, it's the start of the real hard work, not the end of it. The road out of this will continue to be winding and bumpy.

That particular reality is biting for most freelance artists, because they will be the last to feel the benefits of any thaw in the deep freeze. The whole fragile ecosystem needs to return before the freelancer's diet will be sufficient for survival, and there's scant recognition or support from government, nor from the industry that depends on their gifts for its very existence. Some artists have already been lost to the profession for good, and many more are considering their options. The nature of publicity means our audiences won't hear about that until it's too late to help. The government has its eye on other things. The industry needs to do more, and quickly.

But paradigm shifts are hard. For all the talk of the "New Normal", scratch the surface of much of it and you find that what's actually being considered is just the old normal, perhaps with (even) less funding and financial security. We have to do better, think more broadly, and reconsider every aspect of what we do and why.

There are the beginnings of inspiring ideas emerging, all bearing the common imprint of the new, different, reformed, reimagined, enhanced, intensified, liberated; rather than the failing near-exhaustion of the reduced, diluted, the pale imitations of a receding past. Nothing is permanent, and it's our mortality that makes life so precious.

Looking back over the last six months through the prism of these meanderings, it strikes me how many of what seem like specific symptoms of this current crisis are in fact pre-existing weaknesses laid bare. That's what SARS-CoV-2 does to the human body; on a larger scale, that's also what it's doing to the systems humans have created.

You'd hope that Max Planck was wrong, and that old dogs can learn new tricks. To be blunt, the best that we of my generation can do is to keep asking the questions, even - especially - if we have to admit we have few, if any, of the answers. Perhaps the real solutions to these problems can only be conceived by the youngsters who are growing up with them, rather than those that came before. It's difficult for people in positions of authority to consider radically overhauling the system which put them there in the first place.

Meanwhile, I'm still locked down in London. I miss Wales and my family, but I admit that I like it here too. Ashley and her colleagues continue their studies into Covid treatments, striving to chart the shortest course through this for us all. I've been trying to do my bit, volunteering for and helping to publicise various experimental trials, and I've managed to keep her children in one piece, more or less, so far. They've both gone back to school, and are at their happiest for some time. Last week both their class "bubbles" were isolating, which meant a few days of online schooling and lie-ins. They were disappointed at having to stay home. Kids today, eh? I'd have been over the moon in their shoes. Especially when I was a teacher.

I've been working closely with a few composers on valid artistic responses to our current state of affairs. Not *Covid: The Opera*, thank God - ours is an art form which is at its least effective when it's trying to be topical - but sometimes our best work is within the tightest parameters. I hope we'll be able to share some of it with you soon.

And you might have to pay for it, if you can. In compiling this journal for publication, it's provided an instructive parallel that there seems to be a far greater appetite for stumping up for a paperback version than for its digital equivalent, even at double the cost. People, it seems, still like owning *things*.

That's something for the music industry to contemplate, as we work out how we can afford to survive on our ethereal, fleeting sculptures in air.

However long this crisis lasts, we need to develop these overdue new ways of engaging with our audiences, and reaching those who can't necessarily reach us. One way or another, filmed and online content in classical music is here to stay. But we need to work out how to make it pay. Deciding we've had enough of giving it away would be a good start.

24.10.2020

PART TWO

Conversations with Wotan

Introduction

Only two men in history, or so I'm told, have inspired more books to be written about them than Richard Wagner, those being Napoleon and Jesus Christ. From what I know of Wagner, I imagine he'd have objected to being behind at least one of them.

In the autumn of 2018 I found myself, via a long story which I'll save for another time, covering the role of Wotan in the Royal Opera's revival of Keith Warner's production of Wagner's Ring cycle.

I kept a daily diary from the start of rehearsals to closing night, mainly for my own future reference (on the ambitious assumption that I'd be performing the role in my own right sometime soon), but perhaps also with half a mind to producing a publishable version afterwards.

It soon became apparent that wouldn't be happening, although if it had the title might well have been *Breaking Point*, since that is what staging a Ring cycle pushes everyone involved to and sometimes beyond. It was an intense - and, I should say, intensely enjoyable - experience. But one which is probably best left behind closed doors.

By the middle of the performance period I'd been able to take enough of a breath to produce three articles fit for public consumption. I'm including them here just in case Wagner needs that extra push to get past Napoleon.

Why Siegmund?
19th October 2018

Last night I watched a complete performance of *Die Walküre* live for the first time in my life.

This might seem weird to a lot of people with no experience of how an opera singer's life works. I've performed the whole opera on two occasions, scenes from it many times, and have been covering the role of Wotan during the current run of the Ring cycle at Covent Garden. I've also watched its constituent parts, often at some of the world's greatest opera houses and concert halls. If you put together all those bits, you could probably build at least two dozen complete performances, certainly of Acts 2 and 3. And I've listened to or watched it on recordings well over a hundred times. But the fact remains, last night was the first time for me head-to-toe in the flesh.

Viewing it in this new context, it struck me that someone sitting through the Ring cycle with preconceptions might well find it odd that the first instalment, which is tightly wound around the question of the ring, its creation, ownership and power, is abruptly followed by a kitchen-sink drama about Wotan's various families in which the ring seems to play little or no part at all.

What's crucial is what happens between *Rheingold* and *Walküre* (and overlapping from the last part of the former into the first part of the latter) – much of which we can glean from Siegmund and Sieglinde's exchanges during Acts 1 and 2, and Wotan's monologue in Act 2. Here's a stab at joining Wagner's dots.

To recap: during *Das Rheingold*, Wotan's lifelong quest for power is intensified to a dangerous extent by the decision to employ the giants to build a castle – as yet unnamed – for the gods, along with Alberich's recent creation of the ring. The necessity to pay the builders leads Wotan to commit theft, in violation of his own personal moral code, although not the code of contractual law from which he draws most of his current power. That theft leads to his possession of the ring, and his being afflicted by its curse – the nature of which is mutable, but at the very least involves an unshakeable obsession with retaining or reclaiming it.

Wotan's refusal to cede the ring to the giants as part of the payment for the castle leads the gods to the brink of civil war. At which point Erda intervenes – an extraordinary, almost certainly unprecedented act for her, emphasising how extreme the danger is at this point. She tells Wotan two things: that the gods are not immortal, and that he should cede ownership of the ring. (N.B. but not that the latter will avoid the former.)

The news of his own mortality is a shocking revelation to Wotan, as it would be to anyone. *(Rosencrantz: "Whatever became of the moment when one first knew about death? There must have been one. A moment. In childhood. When it first occurred to you that you don't go on forever. Must have been shattering, stamped into one's memory.")* It – and its consequent valedictory from Erda, "sinn' in Sorg' und Furcht!" – is the turning point in his life, his character arc. Does he feel those things in that instant, to their full effect? I suspect not – it's the murder of Fasolt by Fafner, and the realisation that he was moments away from a similar act of familicide himself – that twists the knife of fear which Erda has placed in his heart. ("Urwissend stachest du einst der Sorge Stachel in Wotans wagendes Herz" – *Siegfried* Act 3 Sc 1)

134

Either way, he is now gripped by fear ("Sorg und furcht fesseln den Sinn") *from this point on through the rest of the cycle* – right up until "Ruhe, ruhe, du Gott!" at the end of *Götterdämmerung* – and it is the most fundamental driving factor in all his subsequent actions, despite his best efforts.

"Abendlich strahlt der Sonne Auge" (*Rheingold* Sc 4) is therefore a soliloquy on how fundamentally Wotan has changed from the start of Scene 2 ("Von Morgen") to this point at the end of the opera ("bis Abend") – a change from a state which has remained essentially the same for hundreds, if not thousands, of years. Deep down he realises that the construction of this place was a terrible mistake, and the price was not worth paying. He senses the forces of darkness closing in on him – whether these are real or perceived, internal or external, is very much open to question – and he is seized by his habitual politician's logic. (*Sir Humphrey Appleby: "Something must be done. This is something. Therefore we must do it."*)

Enter the sword motif. ("So grüss' ich die Burg" – Das *Rheingold* Sc 4) The obvious implication is that in this moment the idea of Siegmund occurs to him – perhaps it does, but subsequent events seem to imply that the detailed version is some way off. More likely is that at this point it's a more general idea of war, strife and conflict as a means to defend the gods and reclaim the ring. ("die solltet zu Sturm und Streit ihr nun stacheln, ihre Kraft reizen zu rauhem Krieg" – *Die Walküre* Act 2 Sc 2) This leads Wotan to name the castle: *Walhall*. (Keith Warner points out that this is deliberately not a straight translation of "Valhalla" – the implication being that this castle will not be a luxurious palace, but a fortress, a military stronghold.)

They are going to war.

But against whom? At this point it doesn't matter – the aim is to train and test the mettle of humans, to select the strongest as the heroes who will defend Walhall against any potential invasion. The God of Justice, Honour and Integrity has become a God of War.

But he is still a god gripped by fear, and this draws him to seek out Erda ("wie sie zu enden, lehre mich Erda: zu ihr muss ich hinab!" – *Das Rheingold* Sc4).

(Is there something else too? "Von der Liebe doch mocht' ich nicht lassen, in der Macht verlangt' ich nach Minne." – *Die Walküre* Act 2 Sc 2. Since it doesn't link directly to his lines about Erda, perhaps this yearning for love is more of a wider explanation for his extra-marital affairs, which would certainly seem to support the idea of his marriage to Fricka being primarily motivated by power, not love.)

It's clear that he gleans a lot more from Erda during this second encounter, which occurs at some point between the events of *Rheingold* and *Walküre*, (e.g. "jetzt versteh' ich den stummen Sinn des wilden Wortes der Wala" – *Die Walküre* Act 2 Sc 2: they've clearly talked a lot, as you might expect from these two), and also that Erda gives birth to Brünnhilde as a result.

And also the other Valkyries? Maybe or maybe not – since Wagner doesn't provide any specific information on that one way or the other, we infer that he didn't think it mattered, or wanted us to speculate endlessly about it, or possibly both. Either way, Brünnhilde is clearly exceptional amongst the Valkyries, perhaps because of her mother, perhaps because she's the first-born or last-born, perhaps because Wotan is increasingly aware that the Valkyries and their hero-gathering are not the answer to his problems – and in fact may even be intensifying the danger, by providing

Alberich with a ready-made army to control should he regain the ring. ("der Helden Muth entwendet' er mir, die Kühnen selber zwäng er zum Kampf, mit ihrer Kraft bekriegte er mich." – *Die Walküre* Act 2 Sc 2)

(Is this sudden – and as far as we know, entirely new – urge to beget offspring also a result of the revelation of his mortality? Hell of a coincidence if not.)

It seems that all roads keep leading back to the need for Wotan to regain the ring. (One could argue that this is the curse exerting its influence, or possibly that the 'curse' itself is just a logical extension of the existence of an object that powerful.) But since Fafner gained the ring directly from Wotan as payment for a fulfilled contract, Wotan can't retake it from Fafner by force without destroying the basis of his own power by breaking a contract. ("Was mit den Trotz'gen einst du vertragen, dess' Runen wahrt noch heut' deines Speeres herrischer Schaft: nicht du darfst, was als Zoll du gezahlt, den Riesen wieder entreißen: du selbst zerspelltest deines Speeres Schaft; in deiner Hand der herrische Stab, der starke, zerstiebte wie Spreu'!" – *Siegfried* Act 2 Sc 1)

For me it's an important parameter at several points in the cycle that Wotan could kill Fafner very easily. During *Rheingold* he doesn't fear the giants in their normal form, nor Alberich as a Tarnhelm-induced dragon; he kills the fearsome Hunding with the merest flick of an eyelid – his spear makes him essentially physically invincible. And yet he won't go near Fafner's cave. ("ihn scheut' der Mächt'ge, und meidet den Ort." – *Die Walküre*, Act 3 Sc 1) Why? Because he fears the consequences of a confrontation with Fafner – that he might be tempted to reclaim the ring by force, thus undermining the basis of his own power, and effectively bringing the gods' reign to an end, in the same way that later, as Fricka points out, allowing Siegmund to liberate Sieglinde by killing Hunding would.

So Wotan needs someone to do the dirty work for him, and this agent needs to be very clearly not acting for him – in other words, not merely a blindly obedient extension of his will, in the way that e.g. Brünnhilde and the other Valkyries are, since that would effectively be the same as Wotan killing Fafner himself.

How does he set about creating this free agent? To begin with, he chooses a mortal woman as the mother. (We infer therefore that, even if the other Valkyries are not the offspring of Erda, their mothers must surely be goddesses of some sort.) He then loads Siegmund with the burden of every possible earthly misfortune, including the loss of both parents and his sister. And before abandoning him, he instils in him the practice of defying all society's laws and norms – the laws and norms of the gods. ("Ich weiss ein wildes Geschlecht, nicht heilig ist ihm was andern hehr:" – *Die Walküre* Act 1 Sc 2; "gegen der Götter Rath reizte kühn ich ihn auf" – Act 2 Sc 2)

Surely this man could not possibly be said to be acting as an extension of the will of the gods, when his behaviour is constantly in direct opposition to their long-established desires and intentions?

This is an argument which is, of course, easily demolished by Fricka. ("Du schufst ihm die Noth" – *Die Walküre* Act 2 Sc 1; "So leicht ja entfrug mir Fricka den Trug" – Act 2 Sc 2) Furthermore, it's the mortal nature of Siegmund and Sieglinde's mother which seems to be what really provokes Fricka's ire ("da zu niedrigster Schmach du dich neigtest, gemeiner Menschen ein Paar zu erzeugen" – Act 2 Sc 1) – even though it's the moral outrage of incest which gives her the opportunity to intercede on the moral high ground.

In other words, Wotan's Project Siegmund is undone by the combination of the (necessary) fact of him having a mortal mother, and the (unintended, and unnecessary to the project) existence of a twin sister. That is to say that if Mrs Wälsung had given birth to Siegmund alone, then Fricka would still be irate, but wouldn't have had this opportunity to intervene.

And so what was conceived by Wotan, at and beyond the end of *Das Rheingold*, as an epic project to reclaim the ring and safeguard the future of the gods, is undone by the specific human details of the project's mechanics. The train of power derailed by love.

And that's why, at the beginning of *Die Walküre*, we're suddenly in a very different world to that of *Das Rheingold* – zoomed in on the human consequences of the power games of those above.

19.10.2018

(Afterthought: why does it have to be Siegmund and not Sieglinde? If their mother had given birth to several girls one by one, would Wotan have kept going, Henry VIII-style, until he gained a son? Why Luke and not Leia? The irony being that of course the answer to Wotan's urgent question of who is the free spirit who will return the ring to the Rhinemaidens is under his nose all the time – just that she happens to be female.)

What Wotan Wants
22nd October 2018

"Weißt du, was Wotan will?" – *Siegfried* Act 3 Scene 1

Wagner wrote the vast majority of the text for the Ring between 1848 and 1852, and the music from 1853 to 1876. Around this time physicists (as we would now label them) were putting the finishing touches to the achievements of classical Newtonian physics – the laws of thermodynamics, Maxwell's Equations, kinetic theory and statistical mechanics, and so on – all of which could have persuaded a perfectly rational person to agree with Laplace's sentiments of a few decades earlier, "that if at one time, we knew the positions and speeds of all the particles in the Universe, then we could calculate their behaviour at any other time, in the past or future" (to borrow Stephen Hawking's paraphrased translation).

In other words, the events of the future are entirely determined by those of the past and the present, and if we could somehow know everything about the state of the Universe at this very instant, we could predict every event of the future with the utmost accuracy.

So much for the 1800s. The 20th Century arrived and with it Planck, Heisenberg, Einstein and company, who stumbled upon a load of stuff which meant that the future couldn't be predicted – or, more accurately, that everything about the present couldn't possibly be known in unlimited detail, and therefore there would always inevitably be a degree of uncertainty about the future.

And so the Norns' rope snapped forever.

141

Having said that, the more he thought about it, the more Einstein had grave doubts about the idea that the nature of the Universe was fundamentally non-deterministic: "It seems hard to sneak a look at God's cards. But that He plays dice... is something that I cannot believe for a single moment."

In his 1936 book *An Actor Prepares*, Stanislavski invites us to identify a "super-objective" for our characters, meaning the ultimate goal of the character's actions over the course of the events of the story. This can then be broken down into a series of objectives in individual scenes, each of which usually brings the character closer to his super-objective.

Most singers portraying Wotan in *Das Rheingold* and *Die Walküre* will find identifying his super-objective to be a reasonably straightforward task: after all, he pretty much lays it bare at the start of his 'monologue': "Als junger Liebe Lust mir verblich, verlangte nach Macht mein Muth". Assuming we take him at face value, a super-objective of Power seems pretty unarguable. (Although perhaps Control, as a more active and tangible idea, is potentially a more fertile choice for the actor in practice.)

So far, so good. But over the course of *Die Walküre*, Wotan's shattering realisation is that this all-consuming pursuit of power has come at the most appalling personal cost, and by the end he is a broken man, trudging away from Brünnhilde's fiery mountain top on a long self-flagellating quest for...

Well, for what? That is the question once Wotan has become The Wanderer.

Mime: "Wer ist's, der im wilden Walde mich sucht?"
Alberich: "Wer naht dort schimmernd im Schatten?"

142

Erda: "Wer scheucht den Schlummer mir?"

Wotan spends half his time in this opera being asked who he is, which is always a significant question in Wagner's works. Even more significantly, he seems distinctly undecided as to the correct answer, to the extent that Wagner has even given him a *nom de voix* in the dramatis personae – and this for a character who has up till now shown a marked predilection for name-dropping himself at the slightest opportunity. There's a clear implication that he is undergoing a severe crisis of identity.

The entire Ring cycle is much more concerned with setting us questions than giving us answers – a quality which leads to frustration among its detractors, and often scorn of Wagner's abilities as a dramatist, but which surely goes a long way to explaining the enduring nature of its appeal. In the same spirit, I'll attempt to highlight some – hopefully to some extent enlightening – questions which face the singer as he approaches this third instalment as Wotan.

Early in *Das Rheingold*, her husband assures Fricka that "Wandel und Wechsel liebt wer lebt; das Spiel drum kann ich nicht sparen!": wherever the action is, he just has to get involved. Yet by Act 2 of *Siegfried*, his tune has changed: "Zu schauen kam ich, nicht zu schaffen" he tells Alberich - he's here to observe not to interfere, having seemingly learned the lesson of the confrontation with his wife during *Die Walküre*: that his involvement, however indirect, with the affairs of men can only end in their ruin.

And yet. If he's truly not getting involved, why does he show up at Mime's home – what's his Stanislavskian objective – and why now? What is he hoping to achieve? And what is this business of the riddles all about?

Stanislavski talks of drama as starting with The Magic If. But at times it's just as useful an exercise to ask, "what if not?" In our example, what happens if Wotan doesn't turn up at Mime's right now? It's pretty clear from Act 1 Scene 1 that Mime and Siegfried's relationship is near breaking point, and that the boy intends clearing out the moment the dwarf has managed to forge a half-decent sword for him. It's equally clear that this task is beyond Mime, and likely that this fact will occur to Siegfried at any moment – in which case I think we can speculate with a fair degree of confidence that Siegfried would then dispatch or dispense with Mime, or both, and head off on his gap year travels. Which would presumably mean no Nothung and no slaying of Fafner.

The implication of this is that Wotan's objective in this scene is to ensure that Nothung is reforged and that Siegfried is united with it. And so it's clear that Wotan wants Siegfried to slay Fafner and claim the ring. Is it?

Let's move forward with that in mind. Wotan's next move is to head for Neidhöle itself – a place he has been conspicuously shunning since Fafner set up his distinctly unwelcoming shop there. Why? And why now?

He finds Alberich has beaten him to it, which seems to come as a surprise, and his conversation with Mime's brother leads a winding dance, and ends with Wotan leaving having done nothing other than provoke Fafner, seemingly purely as a wind-up, and tell Alberich to be more like him and chill out.

So again – what if not? What if Alberich hadn't been there? Was Wotan really planning just to be a spectator at Siegfried vs Fafner? To step in if needed? Or to make sure Siegfried didn't fall victim afterwards to Mime's skullduggery? But if that was his plan, what occurs during his conversation with Alberich to make him change it?

Perhaps there's a clue in the name by which he greets his old adversary: "Schwarz-Alberich" – suggesting there's a direct thread in his mind to the man he has just recently recognised as "Licht-Alberich": himself. Is his decision to leave them to it, rather than stay and thus lead himself into the temptation to interfere, an effort to avoid taking further steps down the path to this dark spot in which Alberich finds himself? Bear in mind that at this point they're still the only two people to have had the ring and lost it, united in their uniquely shared knowledge of the curse's burden. Wotan decides to step back: "Wen ich liebe, laß ich für sich gewähren: er steh oder fall, sein Herr ist er" and even "Alles ist nach seiner Art: an ihr wirst du nichts ändern." He has truly, it seems, learned his lesson.

And yet.

Without Wotan's interference, and freely, of his own volition, wielding a weapon forged only by his own ingenuity and need, Siegfried conquers Fafner, gains the ring, and avoids Mime's traps. Which is what Wotan wanted, right? So the next time we see him, he is at peace and triumphant, right?

If that is our hypothesis – and it is an entirely reasonable one – the opening of Act 3 will come as a shock to our system. Its thematic material is familiar, and yet it is quite unlike anything we've heard up to now in the Ring cycle. And it is a world away from depicting a man in contented repose, facing a blissful retirement with benign resignation.

Wotan is summoning Erda for what will be their third and final encounter. His objective this time is clear – he has a question to ask her: "Wie zu hemmen ein rollendes Rad?"

But what wheel? Rolling towards where? At this point in the story, surely he can only mean one thing: the wheel is Siegfried and he is rolling, seemingly unstoppably, towards Brünnhilde. Perhaps Wotan is merely enquiring casually as to whether he truly is unstoppable, just making sure it'll all turn out okay. But the turmoil of the music suggests otherwise – that he really does want to know if there's a way of preventing all this, of turning the tide and restoring the old order rather than let it be swept away.

His turmoil continues into the next scene, where again his behaviour displays no logical consistency – does he really change his entire universal game plan merely as a result of Siegfried pissing him off a bit? Or is the issue with our unreasonable expectation that people should only ever act in accordance with their own stated goals, never against their own interests?

"Do I contradict myself? Very well then I contradict myself; (I am large, I contain multitudes.)" – Walt Whitman

Let's go back to those riddles in Act 1. Why not just turn up and tell Mime that he needs to let Siegfried forge the sword? Well, surely because that would be direct intervention – the consequences of which were demonstrated so brutally in *Walküre*. So Wotan needs to find a way to intervene which would stand up as having nothing to do with his will. And so he arrives at

146

Mime's home, not directly, but having first spent many years wandering the entire world ("Die Welt durchzog ich, wanderete viel" – Act 3 Sc 1) – this is almost the very last place he visits. And as a bedraggled, saddle-sore wanderer, he is sure to be offered, however reluctantly, the hospitality which custom dictates is afforded to weary travellers.

(We've seen this before, remember – when Hunding, also reluctantly, offers the same to Siegmund. Hunding is the champion of Fricka of course, and this sort of moral obligation is very much her realm rather than that of Wotan's contractual law, all of which would no doubt stand Wotan in good stead if challenged once again by his wife or those loyal to her.)

We might conclude therefore that Wotan's objective in this scene is to help Mime without exerting his own will – in other words, to somehow set things up so that Mime asks for his help, in circumstances under which Wotan is morally obliged to give it. The scene would last a couple of minutes at most, were it not for Mime's compulsive biting of the hand with which Wotan is attempting to feed him.

(If those objectives and obstacles are clearly established in the performers' minds then there's a chance of bringing out the genuine situational comedy of the scene, as well as making sense of the fact that it lasts a lot longer than it might at first seem to need to.)

Back to the mountain. Why does Wotan feel the need to meet Siegfried in person at all? It would appear that the Woodbird is doing a perfectly good job of leading him in the right direction, and only abandons him because of Wotan's unsociable ravens. Left alone, surely the wheel would just keep on rolling right to its inevitable destination?

"Wer sagt' es dir, den Fels zu suchen? Wer, nach der Frau dich zu sehnen?"
"Wer reizte dich, den starken Wurm zu besteh'n?"
"Wer schuf das Schwert so scharf und hart, daß der stärkste Feind ihm fiel?"
"Doch, wer schuf die starken Stücken, daraus das Schwert du dir geschweißt?"

This time it's Wotan's turn to ask, who? And the final answer is, of course, himself. However...

Siegfried: "Was weiß ich davon?"

The grandson genuinely doesn't recognise his (paternal and maternal) grandfather. The first part of the test is complete – he truly is the free agent that Siegmund could, tragically, never be.

From now on, though, the conversation gets testier. Perhaps Wotan sinks deeper into the realisation of how different this version is from his beloved Siegmund. Perhaps he rapidly foresees how dismally Siegfried will fare the instant he encounters a world of human politics and intrigue such as the hall of the Gibichungs.

But consider also the information he manages to impart to Siegfried as the encounter becomes more confrontational.

"heut nicht wecke mir Neid: er vernichtete dich und mich!"
"Den Weg, den es zeigte, sollst du nicht ziehn!"
"Fürchte des Felsens Hüter!"
"wer sie erweckte, wer sie gewänne, machtlos macht' er mir ewig."

And so on, followed by a detailed description of what the final stages of the path will look like and the obstacles he will encounter. Sure, he's telling Siegfried what not to do, rather than telling him to do it – but what better way is there of getting a recalcitrant youth to do what you want? Consciously or otherwise, Wotan has hit upon an inspired piece of reverse psychology.

More than that, he could stand up in court and testify perfectly honestly that he has done everything but help Siegfried: in Act 1 he has aided Mime's scheming, in Act 2 (however ineffectively) he has lent a hand to Alberich, as well as warning Fafner and giving him details of the approaching threat, and in Act 3 he has asked the all-knowing Erda how to stop Siegfried himself, having first exhausted every other source of knowledge in the world, and then confronted him in person and done all in his power to halt his progress, up to and including physical violence. "Wie schüf' ich den Freien, den nie ich schirmte, der im eig'nen Trotze der trauteste mir?" At this second attempt he has cracked it.

The character's super-objective may well be unclear, his Stanislavskian through-line hardly a straight one – it is contorted, twisting, and at many points hard to follow at all. It is the path of a man keen to cover his tracks, to set up the probability of a freely-willed outcome, rather than insisting on absolute control over fate and destiny.

It is the behaviour, in other words, of a god who plays dice.

22.10.2018

.

Death of the Hero
24th October 2018

A year ago I was here at Covent Garden watching Strauss' *Salome* for the first time. A few minutes from the end I realised I had no idea how the opera finishes. After doing this job for twenty years you just assume you've seen everything somewhere before, and this is the story of John the Baptist after all – what surprises could it possibly hold? But then it struck me that I wasn't familiar with Strauss' (nor Oscar Wilde's) version, and so the ending – I won't spoil it for you in case you're in the same boat as I was – came as a genuine shock.

You see, I hadn't done my homework.

That's what they tell us, the opera people, isn't it? "Of course it's accessible to everyone, you just need to do your homework beforehand." Because naturally if the audience can't follow what's going on then it must be their fault.

Elsewhere in the dramatic arts, committed fans are increasingly obsessed with avoiding spoilers, in this age of inescapable social media. In other words, they are doing all they can to avoid "doing their homework". By contrast, in the opera business we actively encourage our followers to seek out the spoilers, not for the first time swimming directly against the tide of the rest of modern existence.

Also around this time last year, a load of middle-aged men were up in arms at the revelation in Star Wars: *The Last Jedi* that Rey, the new trilogy's protagonist, was nobody in particular at all – a girl from nowhere, as opposed to the heiress or even reincarnation of a major character from the previous trilogies, as the pre-release betting would have had us believe. (When they're not going to great lengths to avoid spoilers, movie fans spend a lot of time speculating about what surprises forthcoming releases might contain, and then being disappointed when they turn out to be wrong.) In fairness, the trailer for *The Force Awakens* had told us this very thing: "Who are you?" a voice asks; "I'm no-one", Rey answers.

In fact a lot of Star Wars' most ardent fans found a lot more than that with which to take issue in *The Last Jedi*. What was the point, they asked, of long sections of the movie where our heroes set off an a quest which didn't end up in a plucky triumph achieved by a combination of shooting things and the absence of detailed planning?

We're not used to stories about failure, and they're hard for us to understand.

A commentator recently described the effect of the Trump presidency on the US political system as being akin to releasing a horse in a hospital. The same analogy could be used to describe Siegfried's impact on the Gibichung household in *Götterdämmerung*. He is, quite literally, a character from a different opera, and his very existence radically alters the balance of power in this time and place, just as can be said of the ring itself during the events of *Das Rheingold*.

But Siegfried in the real world of politics, power and intrigue is a man way out of his depth. In *Siegfried*, Wagner sets up the eponymous hero as an essentially infallible protagonist, untroubled by setbacks or fear. He sweeps all before him. In the sequel he is as hapless and error-strewn as he was flawless before. "How is this man a hero", many quite reasonably ask, "when he behaves so badly: bigamy, treachery, arrogance, rape, deceit?" - his fall from grace is hard, fast and goes right down to the bottom.

If we approach *Götterdämmerung* with the open mind which Wagner requested of his audience, surely the answer is clear: his heroism evaporates almost instantaneously upon contact with the real world. Or to put it another way, the value of a monomythical hero, even one as all-conquering and indestructible as Siegfried, to us as real humans is precisely zero.

The Ring is a story of failures: Siegfried, Siegmund, Sieglinde, Mime, Alberich, Fasolt, Fafner, Fricka, Erda, Loge, Sintolt and Wittig, the Woodbird, even - and especially - Wotan himself: failures every single one. Siegfried dies alone in a forest, and his funeral march is not so much for him as for what we had hoped he might have been.

And Brünnhilde? Well, she succeeds in reclaiming the ring, returning it to the Rhinemaidens, and wiping the slate clean. But she leaves us with little to go on as to what happens after that.

Keith Warner's current Royal Opera House production of *Götterdämmerung* ends with a figure standing on a giant metal ring, similar in style to the coils we have seen entwined around the set at various points over the course of the cycle, but now reforged into a clean, unsullied circle. Who is this figure? It looks like no-one we've met in any of the four operas.

The Ring is far more about questions than answers, and one big question overrides all others at the end, the question which all theatre as art should leave us with: what next?

Since everyone in the Ring cycle, be they human or immortal, a god or a hero, has failed, who is going to come and save us, to solve all our problems and clean up our mess? Warner's answer seems to be the same one we find in *The Last Jedi*: No-one.

And quite possibly Wagner's too. Bear in mind that the Ring began in conception as a single opera about Siegfried's death, and so everything before *Götterdämmerung* might well be viewed as the set-up for the pay-off – not so much about the death of a hero, but the death, the total demolition beyond any possible hope of a rematch, of the idea of the Hero at all.

No-one's coming to fix this for us, not at this stage of the game. Not at five minutes to midnight. Not at the end of the third act of *Götterdämmerung*. We asked for free will, to be masters of our own destiny, and we got it.

And the upshot of that is that either we learn that we're going to have to solve our problems ourselves, or we're done for.

24.10.2018

Conversations with Wotan
17th December 2014

This article first appeared in the January 2015 edition of 'Wagner News', the journal of the UK Wagner Society, as a report on my activities funded by winning their competition in December 2013.

I don't believe in heroes. Now, you might point out that this is potentially a major problem when starting out on the process of tackling Wagner's body of work, so allow me to elaborate. For an artist, I think role models and inspirations are important, especially early on in one's development, for example when choosing this as a career in the first place. And even the most seasoned singers can learn something new from everyone with whom they share a stage or rehearsal room. But hero-worship, in the sense of an uncritical devotion to one individual, forsaking all others? Not helpful, I would venture, for a career where establishing and developing one's own individual, unique artistic personality is vital.

Having said that, if I had a singing hero, there's no argument that it would be Sir John Tomlinson. I very rarely get star-struck – my father worked in television for thirty years, so when I was growing up I was used to meeting famous faces off the box, and it came to seem a very mundane thing. But when my wife introduced me to Sir John after a performance of *Götterdämmerung* in the most recent ROH Ring cycle, I believe my opening conversational gambit was stammered along the lines of, "Performance to meet you, your magnificent was delighted."

How much more nerve-wracking it was a few months later to stand up in front of a panel chaired by Sir John at the Wagner Society Singing Competition finals, and deliver a chunk of the role with which he has been synonymous for the last three decades. And yet there was also a proportional feeling of security – the sense that, if it failed to come off, it would not be as a result of any lack of knowledge or expertise on the part of the panel; and of course the seal of approval, if it came, would be watertight.

The winners of the Competition get considerable input into how the award is spent – perhaps invested is a better word – on further training for their Wagnerian endeavours. The presence of Sir John on last year's panel was providential from my point of view, because gaining his input had been at the top of my list of priorities from the moment it became clear that there was some merit in my exploring this repertoire. So I was delighted when over a coffee and slice of cake in Antwerp, where he was appearing in Calixto Bieto's new production of *Lady Macbeth of Mtsensk* earlier this year, he agreed to spend some time guiding me through the swirls and eddies of Wotan's journey through *Das Rheingold*.

We met at the Royal Opera House in August for two challenging, fascinating and stimulating afternoons, during which it was my privilege to mine the uniquely rich seams of Sir John's knowledge of the role of Wotan, and of the Ring in general. I was pleased that these first opportunities to gain the benefit of his input came in private, since work behind closed doors is almost always more fruitful – all parties can speak their minds, and the singer can feel free to risk having a go at something new without fear of falling flat on his face in front of an audience. Consequently, much of what passed between us will remain there. Having said that, I will attempt to draw out a few strands from the wealth of information and insight which I hope might be of general interest.

Wotan's Humanity

Approaching Wotan is like approaching Everest for the first time – what strikes you is the scale of the thing. Not only the sheer amount of material and stage time, but the power and stature of the character. So the question uppermost in my mind for some time had been, how do you go about playing a god?

We tackled this question almost immediately, since it rears its head in the matter of Wotan's sleeping state at the beginning of Scene 2 of *Rheingold*. How, I asked Sir John, did he envisage this state? His answer was characteristically forthright and to the point: Wotan is flesh and blood, and his sleep is identical in every way to human sleep. He has powers, and restrictions, rules, boundaries which are characteristic of his godly nature, but having taken those on board, in the moment of portraying him, his thoughts, feelings, cares and emotions are very much those of a human being.

So, to put it simply, he's asleep.

Sir John elaborated that a major feature of Wotan's character is that at any given moment he is single-minded, focused on one thing at a time to the exclusion of all others, and consequently his state of being is extreme in every direction – this as a result, or at least illustrated by, the sacrifice of his eye. So in terms of the portrayal of the character by the actor, this is where the scale comes in: every thought and action must be committed to in full, further than with any other character. But those thoughts and actions are at the same time recognisable as being those of a man of flesh and blood.

Core Resonance and Wagnerian Legato

There is, so the conventional wisdom goes, no such thing as the ideal Wotan voice – anyone coming to it will bring their own particular strengths and weaknesses. As a baritone, there are parts of the role that dip down into areas of the voice which most of my other repertoire leaves unexplored. Perhaps subconsciously dwelling on this, my first few phrases in Sir John's company contained what he termed attempts to "bassify" the voice.

Sir John was very clear that this is not necessary, and indeed harmful to a key aspect of singing the role, which is to establish and maintain a core resonance to the singing, which is always in one place: forward, not too high and never too low. So at the top of the voice, the singer needs to think of the resonance as being lower than you might expect, and at the bottom, it needs to be kept higher – the desired result being that it is always in a consistent, centred place. This facilitates the authentic Wagnerian legato, where there is a consistent tone throughout the vocal line, while at the same time respecting every single aspect of the language – long and short vowels, clear and committed consonants.

As Sir John pointed out, this is why "there are no small roles in Wagner"; because even in a single phrase there is a plethora of aspects to consider, and every vowel, consonant, long note and short note must be take care of. It's easier said than done!

What struck me about hearing Sir John's voice at close quarters for the first time was the delicacy and precision of his 'attacks' – the initial onset of sound at the beginning of each phrase. From further back in an auditorium, it is the power and rich colour of his tone that grabs us, but it's a valuable technical insight to observe the care with which he sets up and initiates that unmistakable voice each and every time.

Sowing the Seeds

While we are blessed with many skilled and knowledgeable Wagnerian conductors, directors and coaches who can guide our steps as novices in the repertoire, what a singer with Sir John's experience can uniquely offer is an insight into what it feels like to stand on stage and live and breathe this character over the course of a whole Ring cycle. The inexperienced *heldenbariton* might be to tempted to take a little lightly the challenge of Wotan in *Das Rheingold* – compared with the two operas that follow, the vocal line is in general less demanding, and the role itself, if laid end-to-end, perhaps only amounts to forty minutes of singing.

Sir John advises caution. "Wotan must be focused on every word everyone else says. He's fighting for survival a lot of the time." The extended concentration this requires – Wotan is on stage almost without interruption for the final two hours or so of the piece – along with the extremities of his emotional state, the heightened clarity of his every thought, mean that the role requires a huge amount of energy and commitment, and should not be underestimated. Sir John left me with the thought that *Das Rheingold* should be viewed as an investment for the singer playing Wotan – one which, if approached correctly, will pay dividends in the two operas which follow.

At the end of our two days we left Wotan just at the point of Erda's entrance in Scene 4. My hope, further funding permitting, is to pick up where we left off with Sir John sometime in the New Year. In the meantime, I have been left with plenty to work on, and the most nourishing food for thought imaginable.

17.12.2014

PART THREE

Orally Fixated:
Postcards from a pre-Covid world

Introduction

I leave you with a lucky dip of other articles from over the years, discussing *Tosca*, diversity in opera, sweets, time travel, and the prophetic powers of fruit machines. That essentially covers all my fields of interest.

There's also the penultimate piece, which I'd really like you to read if you have time, about my stolen *Das Rheingold* score, which as I write is still missing. I have a feeling it's out there somewhere - and the reward for its safe return still stands, in case you ever stumble across a battered old red book of sheet music with my name inside.

If there's a common theme, it's that each chapter gives a glimpse of how the world was before the pandemic, right up to late February 2020. It seems a long time ago.

Why Tosca Dies
3rd November 2019

When opera gets criticised, as it often does these days, for killing its sopranos, *Tosca* is almost always at the top of the list. A virtuous, beautiful, talented, charismatic heroine, manipulated and tormented through no fault of her own, and forced by her scriptwriters to end it all every night of the week in a fatal leap from the top of a Roman landmark. Why? What's the point being made here?

We need to take care when addressing this soprano-killing question. The death of a character is not the same as the death of the singer playing the character – in fact, death scenes are some of the most rewarding to act, and dying on stage should come at no personal risk to the actors involved; and the climactic death of a character very often greatly increases her importance to the narrative – contrast Tosca's death with that of Cavaradossi, or even more so, with poor old Angelotti's.

Having said that, Tosca's demise does seem particularly brutal and unjustified. One could end the show after Act 2 and have a very different, and perfectly satisfactory, story, with a different moral to be drawn. Act 3 arguably seems to subvert the idea of a moral entirely – it feels like a bleakly amoral story, with an almost nihilistically hopeless conclusion.

In fact, even the far-from-faint-hearted Puccini balked at Tosca's death. His preference was for an extended mad scene, Cavaradossi's execution pushing her over the edge mentally rather than architecturally. It was Sardou, author of the play on which the opera is based, who dug his heels in and insisted that only a suicidal denouement would do the job as intended.

167

Tosca is essentially a story about the clash of the contrasting world-views of its three main characters. Cavaradossi: a Voltairian, anti-religion, anti-authority, free-spirited, liberal. (In Dungeons & Dragons we'd have labelled him "Chaotic-Good".) Scarpia: brutal, authoritarian, willing to turn the machinery of State and Church to his own ends of maintaining order and increasing his own personal power. (D&D: "Lawful-Evil".) And caught between them, Tosca herself: pious, law-abiding, altruistic. (D&D: "Lawful-Good".)

I've just arrived in beautiful Inverness, where we're touring Anthony Besch's classic 1980 production of the piece, which updates the action to the summer of 1943. Scarpia and his henchmen are black-shirted, jackbooted fascists, in case anyone was in any doubt whose side we're supposed to be on. The updating was innovative and not without controversy when Besch and his designer Peter Rice first deployed it; by now it seems a familiar idea. But having said that, this time around (this being the third revival I've been involved in since I started my professional career here with Scottish Opera in 2004) there seems to be a certain added energy and edge to the concept, and to the audience reactions. At first we wondered why that was; I suspect at least part of the answer might be found by opening any current newspaper.

One of the many remarkable things about this piece is the tautness of its construction – Act 2 in particular hangs together with the undeviating tension of a well-tuned piano string. Scarpia and Tosca initially meet in the Roman church of Sant Andrea della Valle, where in this production Rice made sure that the mural of St Andrew being crucified in saltire formation is unmissably upstage centre. (A canny piece of subliminal wooing of his Scottish audience, perhaps.) From that first moment, Scarpia zeroes in on two

168

aspects of Tosca's personality – her piousness and her jealousy – to manipulate her into unwittingly leading him to the hiding place of the escaped political prisoner Angelotti. Given that he is being concealed by Cavaradossi, Scarpia also concocts a plan to use the latter's legal predicament to blackmail Tosca into granting him sexual favours.

This plan is essentially watertight – during Act 2, Scarpia even gives Tosca a tour of the various strands of his spider's web, demonstrating to her that she is comprehensively snared. He fails to identify her one viable escape route – the one she eventually uses – because he assumes that, being a devout and orthodox Catholic, she won't murder him (even if he believes her physically capable of such an act in the first place), since in her mind it would undoubtedly condemn her to Hell. He thinks nothing of abusing her piety against her, but fails to appreciate that her relationship with God is far more direct than the average Roman's, and that she feels He might be willing to bend the rules in her case. In fact, the clues are there in Act 1, when Scarpia chides her for swearing in church, and she replies that God will make an exception for her. For Scarpia it's a fatal and uncharacteristic oversight, but presumably his mind is on other things at this point. Either way, he underestimates her.

If we're to get to the bottom of this story, it's crucial to recognise the nature of Scarpia's power. He is not superhuman, is not physically stronger nor necessarily more intelligent than his opponents. What he does have is the entire machinery of State and Church at his disposal, and an absolute lack of any moral or ethical restraint in using them to satisfy his own desires. On an individual level, Tosca does find the physical and moral resources to defeat him, and if we ended the opera after Act 2 we'd go home thinking this was all that was required. But the moral of the story, if we choose to look for one, is this: it's not enough to depose, imprison or even kill a tyrant. It's the system that gets you, and an individual can't fight an entire tyrannical system and win.

And so, as we face a generational struggle with the question of authoritarian tyranny and how to oppose it, *Tosca* tells us that while it's tempting to focus on the individuals at the top of their authoritarian trees – that, after all, is what their egos demand of us – if we are truly to defeat them, we need to take care to restrain, reform or even dismantle the systems which put them there, and which they would use to keep us under their tyranny.

Let's not allow her nightly deaths to be in vain.

3.9.2019

Home Truths
6th February 2019

There's a moment in Mike Volpe's stunning documentary *Hip Hop to Opera* where his group of teenage schoolkids from south London get treated to an aria by Simon Shibambu – the first time that most of them have heard an opera singer live. (Six minutes in if you find the video online, but take the time to watch the whole thing if you haven't seen it already.) They're asked for their reaction, and once the initial shock has settled down, the first thing they want to know is, how did he end up standing there in front of them as a professional opera singer at the Royal Opera?

Down the road at English National Opera, their new chief executive Stuart Murphy has been giving the industry a public self-flagellation on its lack of diversity in casting, promising to redress the balance via some positive discrimination. For some reason he appears only to apply this principle to the company's singers, no mention being made of a similar policy being applied to the orchestra, technical staff or administrational team – perhaps his offer of resigning in favour of a BAME chief executive went unreported – but I'm sure he didn't intend to give the impression that the important thing is that the company is seen to be diverse, rather than actually being so at every level.

Unfair of me to pick on Mr Murphy – at least he's been brave enough to raise the issue. So let's be just as courageous and bite the bullet: is the UK opera industry racist?

First things first. If you'd stood here in 2015 and told me that British society in general had reached a hermetic state of benign enlightenment, then if you'd happened to catch me in an optimistic mood I might well have been tempted to believe you. After the ongoing events of the last three years, maybe less so now. And it would be a brave soul who claimed that the opera business is somehow immune from the malaises of society as a whole.

That broader topic is for another time though. Apart from society's prejudices, and those of individuals in positions of power within it, what is it about the opera industry in particular which places barriers in the path of Black, Asian and other non-white Minority Ethic (BAME) singers?

(NB I'm using the term BAME for want of a better one, while being aware that its use is not without its controversies.)

Talking to British BAME colleagues, those barriers very often seem to point back to something else, which tallies with my own experience of the business: class.

In that scene from *Hip Hop to Opera*, Simon Shibambu answers by saying that he started singing at 8 years old at home in South Africa, with choirs as a boy soprano. He says there were challenges – that in South Africa classical music is not something many families would want their child to start singing. "Same here", replies one of the south London lads.

"Same here."

The thing is this. Now more than ever, with the current state of the education system in this country, I find it easier to envisage a black South African 8-year-old ending up twenty years later as a professional opera singer than I do an innately talented 8-year-old at a typical British state school. That's not directly to do

172

with ethnicity – although I'm taking the liberty of assuming that if I put on a production of a student opera with an entirely BAME cast, and it turned out all of them had wealthy parents and had studied at expensive private schools and St John's Cambridge, you wouldn't be congratulating me on solving our problem.

At the same time as demanding more young people from less privileged backgrounds climb the long, steep ladder which leads to a professional opera career, we're hacking away at the bottom rungs of that same ladder by cutting back, and often cutting altogether, the provision for music education in state schools. Anyone who is serious about tackling this issue as anything more than superficial window dressing will surely be looking at that end of the process first and foremost, and, given that developing opera singers properly takes at least 20 years, will be setting goals for diversity which are long-term – that is, a process over decades rather than months.

That's not to say that more immediate steps can't be taken, and if UK companies are minded to back the many excellent British BAME singers they already have available to them then that can only be a positive thing. In terms of providing inspiring role models to future generations, if that's what we're after, a home-grown singer surely carries a lot more weight than one who grew up abroad, since their answers to the question "How did you end up here?" have far more chance of being directly relevant and applicable. Opera companies the world over are notorious for being inclined to import solutions to their casting challenges, but there are rewards in the short and long-term for those notable exceptions who strike a balance by investing in local artists too.

Last week on social media I raised the need for UK companies to back home talent in general, especially given the current perfect storm of uncertainty facing UK artists hoping to work anywhere abroad in the near future (not to mention the need to minimise carbon footprints). The hackles of some non-UK singers were immediately raised. There's an instant assumption that more work for UK singers means less for others. Need that be the case? Must we always be a bunch of bald men fighting over the last comb? Backing home-grown singers could mean devising new, additional projects, perhaps addressing Britain's cultural relationship with the rest of the modern world – Lord knows, we could do with examining that somehow. I recently workshopped Guto Puw's new piece for Music Theatre Wales, written in Welsh for two singers and a 12-piece orchestra – hardly prohibitive in budget allocation, therefore – and it's one of the few times where I've felt part of an art form embedded in my own culture, that the concept of 'Welsh opera' meant something significant and tangible, in the way that Italian, German, French, Russian singers must presumably feel every day.

"Same here."

There's something fundamentally important in this process of producing new works in the overcoming of the cultural barrier which stands between British state school kids and traditional opera. Singing ability is, to some large extent, transferable between genres – is it legitimate to insist that, for instance, a talented young black vocalist sings music written by dead white male foreigners, rather than something with a far more direct connection to her own life experience? New music has a critical role to play in bridging that gap – or could have, if we assume that we're interested in producing new pieces that are genuinely useful to contemporary society.

Let's raise another factor, which is that training as an opera singer continues to become ever more eye-wateringly expensive, even compared to other forms of higher education, while the potential financial rewards of the career at the end of it decrease in both size and stability. My sincere advice to anyone thinking of pursuing it as a career, unless they are of independent financial means and/or have a passport from another EU country is: think again, much harder. We're turning what was the most working-class field in classical music into a rich kid's pastime, and no-one seems to be lifting a finger to change that.

A word of warning too for young singers who have managed to make it through to the professional world. The opera business is a machine which is more than capable of chewing singers up, spitting them out, and forgetting about them. And the time to be most on your guard is when the industry decides that it needs you. That's not to say you shouldn't take advantage when it does – we're the ones who sail the boats, and assuming they're seaworthy we'd be foolish not to launch them whenever we find that the tide is in our favour. If, in the interests of 'authenticity', the machine were suddenly to decide that Mr Gedge the vicar had to be played by a middle-aged Welshman, I'd have my diary open before you could say "but you've always hated *Albert Herring*".

In actual fact what you should be saying is "are you sure that's the right role for you vocally?", because these days it certainly isn't. Experienced colleagues won't need me to tell them this, since they're best-placed to make the call themselves, but younger singers should be wary: don't assume that because you're offered a role, you must be capable of singing it right now – in practice, it's not a casting director's job to be the impartial judge of what's in your long-term interests. The industry has suddenly decided that it needs non-white faces on stage – no doubt that's a noble sentiment, but it doesn't mean you're obliged to damage your long-term career and vocal health by pushing your voice into things it shouldn't be doing. Look after yourself, take care, and good advice from a handful of people you trust. You don't owe the machine anything.

Let's leave Mr Gedge to one side for now and consider the role of Otello. Ever since Shakespeare's version of the character became largely – and quite correctly – the preserve of black actors, there's been a clamour from the industry and outside for the same principle to be applied to Verdi's.

The problem isn't that the role that Verdi wrote isn't singable by a black tenor – it's that it isn't really singable by a mortal human being: it's a notorious voice-wrecker, and if a tenor can avoid singing it they probably should. But the machine is desperate for a black Otello, and so any young black tenor immediately has this burden of expectation thrust upon him as soon as he sets foot on stage with a degree of promise – even when he might well be a more suitable Cassio or Roderigo in the same piece. Being a tenor is hard enough as it is, or so they tell me, persistently and loudly.

For the time being the machine has, it seems, decided to solve the problem by casting non-ethnically-specific Otellos, without any hint of "blackface" make-up. Since Verdi's opera is really far more about jealousy than race – much of the subtlety of Shakespeare's treatment of the latter subject is lost in the inevitable contraction that happens when a long play is adapted as an opera libretto – it's probably a legitimate solution of sorts. That only leaves us needing to find answers to the issues presented by Aida, Butterfly, Turandot, Carmen... Perhaps we're going to need a bigger boat.

A senior colleague recently recounted to me that, when about to appear as Wotan for the first time, he'd received some pretty intimidating correspondence objecting to the idea of a black man portraying a character based heavily on Odin. (Who was, according to the letter-writers, unambiguously Aryan... I suppose man creates all sorts of gods in his own image.) Humanity being what it is, we need to take care about well-intentioned initiatives – it rarely takes much for less benign souls to pick them up and use them as a stick with which to beat their customary targets.

Diversity on British stages. Let's return to two questions, both of which boil down to equality of outcome versus equality of opportunity.

If, as a quick fix to diverse casting, the non-white singers on stage are all imported, does that solve our problem? In the context of British opera, how inspiring is a cast of – for example – singers from abroad and Oxbridge choral scholars in terms of laying the foundations for future generations? Ethnicity is a factor in relatability, sure – but if the message we're sending is that BAME singers can make it in opera, as long as they're not born in Britain, then are we any further along a road which leads anywhere useful?

Even more importantly: any competent casting department could quite easily put together an ethnically diverse team from current British talent for most standard operas. Seeing them on stage might well inspire a new generation of youngsters to pursue training in classical music.

But if those youngsters then head back to schools where we are at the very same time removing most, and in many cases all, of the already inadequate training in music and the dramatic arts, is it not just another example of our older generation asking young people why they aren't climbing a ladder which we've already chopped up for firewood?

6.2.2019

Orally Fixated
14th January 2018

Last month the New Yorker published a short story called *Cat Person*, which went viral as part of the ongoing discussion of relations between the sexes. It's a good read – you can still access it online if you're one of the six people who haven't read it, or one of the two people who don't have an opinion on it.

If you're like me* then on first reading you'll have struggled to get past the end of the first paragraph, which mentions Red Vines – which we immediately infer from context to be a kind of confectionery.

Here's the thing. I really like sweets. To the extent of having them organised into a clear hierarchy at all times. (For example: a box of Celebrations goes Malteasers – Galaxy – Galaxy Caramel – Snickers – Mars – Bounty – Milky Way.) Maybe this comes from having two brothers, which necessitated swift decision-making when a tub of chocolates was being passed round at home.

I dutifully read the rest of the story, but the only issues my mind was willing to grapple with on this first pass were related to the revelation of the existence of Red Vines. What are they? What do they look like? What do they taste like? How much do they weigh? (Since the context is that of a cinema sweet shop, that latter point comes into play at the pick & mix stand.) From the name, I guessed that they might be like strawberry laces but thicker – it seemed like a strange choice of snack for a grown man, but that was fairly clearly an inference that the author intended the reader should draw.

Luckily, as with all my innermost thoughts these days, the first thing I did was to post this question on Twitter, and only a day or two later a friend duly presented me with a box of Red Vines. Consequently I am able to inform you that they do look like thicker versions of strawberry laces, but the taste is considerably different – as a taste-texture combination they are something like a Ralgex-flavoured condom.

Clearly, therefore, the type of snack chosen by some sort of psychopath. Bingo! I felt ready to proceed onto the second and subsequent paragraphs of the story.

In fact, if I paid more attention to TV on the rare occasions when I'm actually watching it then I'd have had this Damascene moment a lot sooner. In the series *Fringe* there's a quite brilliant piece of double character work by the Australian actor John Noble, portraying two versions of a scientist named Walter Bishop – the series is set in parallel universes (it's science fiction, did I mention that?), and so each actor is required to play the same character whose circumstances have diverged at some earlier point. It's a forensic measure of acting ability, and Noble is stunning as both Walter Bishops. The Walter Bishop in the show's principal universe is clinically insane, and one of the ways in which this is delineated (by contrast with sane Walter in universe number 2) is his predilection for – you've guessed it – Red Vines.**

I have to admit that my experience reading *Cat Person* was not atypical of my life as a reader. I've read every single Maigret novel, and yet I couldn't tell you a single detail about any of the plots except that he often goes into a bar for a marc, and they are always ordering beer and sandwiches from over the road when they're in the middle of an long interrogation (come to think of it, for

Parisian policemen, that probably just means anything over 10 minutes).

Thomas Hemsley always claimed that years spent singing, as well as the time and effort spent studying and thinking about singing, caused an overdevelopment in the part of the brain concerned with the mouth – teeth, lips and tongue included. This, he speculated, was at least one of the reasons behind the connection between singers and food. It's a plausible theory – I can't think of a singer who doesn't have a passion for eating, drinking, cooking, or combinations thereof. It may also be why you'll still see some singers smoking more often than you'd expect (which is obviously never), and why – based entirely on anecdotal evidence – singers are excellent kissers, although I'll largely leave that to you to explore further if I may.

By the way, Hemsley also used to claim that singers eating a lot was entirely acceptable since in a typical performance a singer would burn more calories than a coal miner during a day's work. Now, I'm the last person to tell people how to do their jobs, but I might suggest that if a singer is expending more energy during two hours on stage than a collier on a 12-hour shift, then they might want to consider calming down a little.

Come to think of it, characters in opera are often required to eat and/or drink during a scene – it doesn't happen in every opera admittedly, but when you take into account that it's the one thing we're literally not able to do while carrying out our job, then it makes absolutely no sense for operas to take place during mealtimes at all. It seems that composers and librettists share their singers' oral fixation.

Which brings us to Freud, who as you might expect had rather a lot to say on the subject of oral fixations. It

181

should be no surprise to you either that Freud was inclined to think that all this was to do with experiences in very early childhood.

So which is it – if Freud is right, perhaps infants with an abnormal experience of breast feeding are more likely to go on to become professional singers? Or do we go with the Jones-Hemsley theory that it's the experience of singing which leads to a more general oral fixation?

Not wanting to leave you hanging, I asked a friend who is a clinical psychologist for her verdict. Her thoughts on Freud: "Some good concepts, twisted by him being a misogynistic sex-obsessed man of his time."

And what about Jones? "Well. You're not a misogynist."

So there you have it. Jones 1, Freud 0. I'm off to crack open a box of Red Vines to celebrate.

14.1.2018

NB you're probably not. Be grateful.

*** Since writing this I've learned that 'The Big Bang Theory' also deals with this subject, Red Vines being Sheldon Cooper's confectionery of choice. (It's quite likely I've also seen this and immediately forgotten about it. I don't watch TV very closely, you may have gathered.) Red Vines = sociopath must be a whole semester on the standard American Creative Writing course.*

Where are all the Time Travellers?
19th June 2020

In 2009, Stephen Hawking held a party in Cambridge. No one came. After the event, he sent out invitations to time travellers from the future to attend. Since none of them had shown up, he claimed this as experimental evidence that time travel is not possible.

He raises a fair question: if time travel is possible, then where are all the time travellers?

Hawking's light-hearted experiment is far from conclusive, of course. Here are four possible reasons for the absence of visitors from the future, one or more of which might explain the no-shows.

1)   Time travel takes a lot of energy.

Science fiction focuses on the idea of sending actual people, bodies and all, back in time. It's obviously a great advantage from a storytelling perspective, but viewed scientifically, it makes little sense.

"That meeting could have been an email." These days we don't, as a rule, send people halfway around the world on an aeroplane when a video conference works just as well. Why? Energy.

The argument holds up even more strongly with time travel, which we'd have to assume would be far trickier – and, without entering into the possible mechanics of it, more energetic – than geographical travel.

An extraterrestrial observer of Earth might ask, "If humans have discovered nuclear technology, then where are all the nuclear explosions?" If time travel turns out to be as energetic and potentially dangerous, it's perfectly conceivable that it will be regulated by the same sort of restrictions we place on nuclear power and weaponry. Hence no trips to Cambridge 2009 for a party, however congenial the host.

2) Time travel kills the time traveller.

Let's run with this energy idea. We'd rather send an email or text message than a human messenger carrying bits of paper. For similar reasons, it's not really plausible that we'd send an actual human back in time. Presumably at some point in the process we'd have to disassemble the molecules of the traveller's body and put them back together. Putting aside the Trigger's Broom question of whether that would actually be the same person, or just a copy, I struggle to think of a method via which ripping someone's entire body apart to the level of individual molecules wouldn't kill them.

Okay you say, but what if we could digitise consciousness, and send that back in time, to be placed in another brain and body, whether that would be artificial or some sort of permanent or temporary donor? In that case, you'd still be left with the original person at the transmitting end of the process – effectively, you've produced a clone, rather than an actual time traveller.

So if the process leads to the death, or at least the problematic cloning, of a human being, it's not something you'd do for frivolous reasons.

In fact, the more you think about it as a serious proposition, the less sense it makes that you'd decide to send an actual human back in time, whether you're talking about their entire body or just their consciousness. Why not just send a message? What are you trying to achieve?

Which brings us to our third question.

3) What's the point?

So it's likely that time travel would be a difficult, costly (in terms of energy and money), and dangerous process. The question would therefore be: what's the object of the exercise?

Again, with the aim of constructing interesting stories, science fiction tends to concentrate on a "many-worlds" or "multiple timelines" approach, where a time traveller can go back to a point in history and change something, thereby altering the future and perhaps avoiding some global catastrophe.

Our experience of time doesn't really back that up though. The past has already happened. If time travellers have gone back in time, whatever the consequences of their actions, we're already living with them. It's a tricky concept for us to accept on a philosophical level – what becomes of free will for those time travellers, if whatever they do leads to a future which they know is already fixed? But that's more of a problem for us rather than Physics – from the point of view of the latter, a "fixed single timeline" model makes far more sense. Indeed, quantum physicists are finding and discussing instances of potential "retrocausality" – events in the present being determined by events in the future. Free will may not come into it, on a subatomic level at least.

"One of the major problems encountered in time travel is not that of becoming your own father or mother. There is no problem in becoming your own father or

mother that a broad-minded and well-adjusted family can't cope with. There is no problem with changing the course of history—the course of history does not change because it all fits together like a jigsaw. All the important changes have happened before the things they were supposed to change and it all sorts itself out in the end." – Douglas Adams, *The Restaurant at the End of the Universe*

If that is the case, then you'd have to ask: what exactly would be the point of travelling backwards in time? If history can't be changed, then what is there to be gained in a perilous and costly trip to visit it?

Any or all of these might well be a factor. But there's one more point which provides sufficient explanation on its own.

4) Time travel requires a receiver as well as a transmitter.

When Alexander Graham Bell invented the telephone, he didn't immediately have the ability to contact anyone in the world remotely. He could only talk to the one man who also had a telephone. Since that's a far simpler process than time travel, why wouldn't the same principle hold?

Again, science fiction is largely fixated on the ability to send people back to any point in space and time. But how would that location be identified and fixed – especially the spatial element? It would clearly require a second set of equipment, which by definition hasn't been invented yet. Just as Professor Bell couldn't call anyone who lived beyond the reaches of his nascent telephone network, so time travellers can't reach any location where time travel hasn't been invented yet, because there's no one to pick up the phone.

In other words, time travel into the past is – or should I say, will be – only possible as far as the point in history at which time travel is invented, and not before. And that's why no one came to Professor Hawking's party.

19.6.2020

Trigger's Missing Brooms
29th February 2020

What's it like being a singer? A lot of it is impossible to explain. If you happen to be reading this on crowded public transport, in a state of mild paranoia about contracting COVID-19, bear in mind that this is how it feels for us all the time. And you wondered why we're all a bit loopy.

Two weeks ago, back in the days when Coronavirus was still a distant problem on the other side of the world, two of my bags were stolen in London – one where I keep my laptop and most of my other electronic equipment, and another where I keep the day's music, usually including my iPad, which is I assume what caught this thief's eye.

The remarkable thing about modern electronics is how instantly replaceable they all are, the cost being almost purely financial. When I spilled an entire cup of steaming hot coffee over my previous laptop, the swift migration of its brain to its replacement (the memory chips having by some miracle survived the 100% Arabica deluge) was so comprehensive that, when I switched it on, its first question was: Your last session was interrupted. Would you like to continue where you left off? (Nice of it to leave out "you clumsy oaf".) Even more seamlessly, my new iPad only required me to place my iPhone beside it to get up and running as if it had been a family member for years. 21st Century computers are Ships of Theseus (or, according to taste, Brooms of Trigger), but even more so, being replaceable in their entirety at one stroke and yet within moments becoming indistinguishable from their instantly-unlamented predecessors.

That's less the case with some other things. A couple of items (including the music bag itself) were gifts from dear friends. And the three vocal scores... perhaps only a singer can really understand what they contained: not so much the printed content, but what had been painstakingly added to them. My *Rake's Progress* with notes from the first outing of the David McVicar production. Stephen McNeff's *The Burning Boy*, with personal contributions from the composer ahead of its world premiere. And most painfully of all, my bog-standard, dog-eared Schirmer economy edition of *Das Rheingold*. Notes from when I first dabbled in some casual Donner over a decade ago, through to some far-more-serious Wotanning over the last couple of years. Insights and anecdotes from John Tomlinson and Willard White. Tempi and dynamics from Tony Pappano and Anthony Negus. Thoughts and interpretations from Keith Warner and Julia Burbach. Language notes, performance advice, stylistic tips, advice, input, support from hundreds of hours of rehearsals and coaching sessions with world-class colleagues, many of them among the greatest living experts on this repertoire. Worthless to pretty much anyone else; priceless to me.

It makes me wish my burglars had been smarter, realised this and contacted me with a ransom note. I can't even imagine what my bottom line would be, but it's almost certainly more than they got for the iPad at least. Only a few months ago I'd had my four Ring cycle scores hardbound, with the idea that they should last me another twenty years at least. As I relinquished them, the bookbinder noticed me getting slightly dewy-eyed, and she said "Don't worry – we'll look after them. We understand better than anyone how much they must mean to you."

I suppose that if the Ring teaches us anything, it's that we shouldn't get too attached to things: however precious an object might seem to us, when our time with it is done, we need to let it go. When I was still training as a singer, a director once challenged me about the fact that I don't take notes in rehearsal. I replied that, since I can't take a notebook out on stage with me, if I can't remember a note then it's no use to me, and if I can remember it there's no point writing it down. (I often miss that younger version of me, with his much more elastic brain, not to mention his largely unfounded overconfidence.)

And having now performed the role of *Rheingold* Wotan, the important, the useful stuff is in my head, and anything I've forgotten, by implication, wasn't worth retaining. If it had been my score of *Walküre*, which I start rehearsing for the first time in a full production just over a month from now, I'd have been in much deeper trouble. And I'm physically unharmed and healthy, I still have a roof over my head and a dry floor under my feet. There are people with far worse problems, coping with losses infinitely greater than mine.

A further silver lining came in the shape of a *Rheingold* score from a second-hand bookshop. The advertised description bore so many uncanny similarities to mine that I thought and hoped it might turn out to be the same one. In fact, it's a distinctly superior version: a beautiful vintage Schott edition, bound in an almost identical way to mine, with unmarked, pristine pages. (It seems originally to have been the property of James W Marshall, organist of St Cuthbert's Church in Darlington and founder of Darlington Choral Society. But rather intriguingly the edition was first published in 1899, three years after his death.) I'm very happy to have made its acquaintance, and at a bargain price.

There's also an argument that leaving some (literal and figurative) baggage behind isn't an entirely negative process, especially with a character who gets under your skin and inside your head as insidiously as this one inevitably does. At the end of Scene 2 of *Rheingold*, Wotan (the way I play it at least) comes to realise that he didn't need Freia's apples after all – his strength and energy come from elsewhere, from within. Sometimes it's only by losing something that we learn how much we can do on our own.

But having said all that, I would love that old score back. If you could keep an eye out for it in charity shops and second-hand bookstores while you're out and about, I'd be very grateful. And if you could remember to sneeze into a hanky and wash your hands regularly while you're at it, that would be even better.

29.2.2020

Let 'em Spin
20th October 2016

March 1996. I'm a trainee physics teacher and we're on a Maths and Science department outing to London, ostensibly to assess various venues for their suitability for school trips. It's also an excuse for a bit of a party (hard-earned over the course of a tough year), and at an early stage of the evening we find ourselves in the Nag's Head, opposite the back of the Royal Opera House in Covent Garden.

Through the fog of hindsight I'm never quite sure when I decided I wanted to be a professional singer. It can't have been earlier than when I was 13, when I first started singing solos as a baritone, and was certainly no later than 23, when I applied to music colleges. What's clear is that the idea must have been quite well-formed in my mind by this point, at the age of 21, because I shove a pound in the Nag's Head fruit machine and tell myself that if I win anything, it means I'm going to sing in the opera house across the road one day.

On the fifth spin the reels stop on three bunches of purple grapes. The machine pays out.

I finally bit the bullet and started music college in the autumn of 1998, and if you'd asked me then to estimate when I would be ready for my Covent Garden debut, I'd have said, with absolute certainty, that it should come as soon as possible, since I was ready right now, or would be very shortly. In those days I wasn't shy of backing my ability, even though that (usually misplaced) confidence would frequently get me into trouble.

Andy Warhol once said that no-one gets anything until they stop wanting it. And things tend to come along, if you're fortunate, when you're actually ready for them, rather than when you think you deserve them.

11am, Tuesday 4th October 2016. I set foot on the stage of The Royal Opera House for the first time, as a Guest Artist in their new production of *The Nose*. It feels like a significant milestone – I walked past the Nag's Head on the way to the stage door, and I'd thought of those three grapes. I look around for a colleague to share the moment with. Perhaps I could tell John Tomlinson, since I'm pretty sure he'd at least feign interest, but he's nowhere to be seen. Everyone is – understandably – preoccupied with their own tasks. I try to take the auditorium in, and check a few basic sight lines, and I put the milestone to one side. In actual fact, perhaps I'm a little disappointed at the lack of thrill inside me; reputation and history aside, it's just another theatre, albeit a very pretty one; by now I've seen a lot of them, and most of them work the same way.

11.05am. I'm standing centre stage. We're in the middle of Act 2 Scene 9, at the beginning of which I have a short solo. The rehearsal has stopped just after my solo ends. The director is shouting at me through a microphone. I'm not in the light. I need to get further downstage. It means reworking my positions completely, ditching what we've been doing for the last four weeks on the dummy set in the rehearsal room. Fine, I'm sure I can deal with that. Thumbs up. Now the conductor is shouting at me. He has a microphone too. I'm singing too fast and not following his beat. I was looking straight at him but there are bright lights shining in my eyes, I'm wearing a prosthetic nose which is slightly too big and a peaked cap which is slightly too small, and it's hard to argue when everyone has a microphone except you. There are ten of my colleagues on stage with me, others in the wings, and an auditorium dotted with people. All of them are very good at their jobs. This is Covent Garden. If you're screwing it up, the chances are it's not someone else's fault.

We start the scene again. I stand in the light and manage to sing at something resembling the right speed. This time we don't stop after my bit and the scene continues. This means it wasn't a total disaster the second time. I think. I go up to my dressing room and sit down. I've worked for eighteen years for this, I'm good at my job and I know my role backwards, and I wanted it to be perfect. I feel like crying but I don't. I pick up the score, look at the awkward corners – frankly, the whole damn piece is an awkward corner – and get to work.

When you're young you tend to undervalue experience, since it's something you don't have and there's no shortcut to obtaining it. You can sing, you can act, you're pretty, you're working on your languages, you know your way around a stage. The operatic world is crying out for a talent like yours. What more could experience bring, other than grey hair and wrinkles and cynicism? I guess what I'm saying is that what experience brings is the capacity to get shouted at by men with microphones and carry on doing your work, screwing it up a little less each time. Or at the very least, screwing it up in more interesting ways.

The Nose opens tonight. It's a very special show, in a very special place, and I'm very proud to be a small part of it. And if you're lucky enough to have a ticket, and have a moment to spare beforehand, feel free to put a pound in the Nag's Head fruit machine for me.

20.10.2016

Follow the author online at:

www.facebook.com/paulcareyjones
www.twitter.com/paulcareyjones
www.soundcloud.com/paulcareyjones
www.youtube.com/paulcareyjones

Read more from the author online at:

www.paulcareyjones.wordpress.com

www.paulcareyjones.net

Printed in Great Britain
by Amazon

49282643R00129